C000285893

hug me while
i weep for i weep
for the world

hug me while i weep for i weep for the world

BEL LITTLEJOHN

Edited by Craig Brown

LITTLE, BROWN

For Asya, Hugh, Oliver and Marius
and in memory of John Wells

A *Little, Brown* Book

First published in Great Britain by
Little, Brown and Company 1998

A CIP catalogue record for this book is available
from the British Library.

A number of these pieces have already appeared, in
slightly different form, in the *Guardian* newspaper.

ISBN 0 316 64716 0

Printed and bound in Great Britain by
Clays Ltd, St Ives plc

Little, Brown and Company (UK)
Brettenham House
Lancaster Place
London WC2E 7EN

for Cherie and Tony and the kids

contents

thanx, guys

Writing a book, as every true writer knows, is like having a baby. My thanks, then, to all those whose courage, fortitude, another word for courage and great good humour have helped me through the ordeal of conceiving and delivering this baby – this occasionally tormented, often challenging, sometimes haunted, and always deeply disturbing baby.

As any sensitive reader will notice, I carried this baby against a backdrop of desperate emotional and political upheavals. Many of the chapters were written while I was suffering from a very, very, bad cold, and the last fifty or so pages were penned under the shadow of catarrh. I nearly sprained my ankle somewhere between pages 55 and 67, and a sore throat, chapped lips and a blocked nose hampered progress in much of the middle section.

So thanks, thanks and more thanks to those who stood by me while I chiselled my way through every chapter, every word, every letter, with my bare hands. The Rt. Hon. Chris Smith generously checked and double-checked the manuscript for maximum creativity, excitement and impact. Thanks, too, to my good chum Anita Roddick for keeping me in tea and sympathy – not to mention her endless supplies of Body Shop Peppermint and Anchovy Foot Lotion for when times got really hard. The Rt. Hon. Jack Straw provided, as always, a shoulder to cry on, and The Rt. Hon. Peter Mandelson gave up a lot of his precious time to read and where necessary amend the text to keep it in line with government policy.

Thanks are also due – in no particular order – to William Blake, Janet Street-Porter, Roger Waters, David Leigh, Martin Luther King, Woody Guthrie, Margaret Beckett, David Helfgott, Pablo Picasso, Carla Lane, Sylvia Plath, Mahatma Gandhi, David Rowan, Gillian Wearing, Barbara Follett, Kahlil Gibran and Bob Dylan for providing inspiration and spiritual nourishment. Love you all to bits.

'Nuff said.

B.L.
London, September 1998

ix

I don't want an old social order. I want a new one, with rules for today . . . a young country, a new Britain.

from *New Britain: My Vision of a Young Country*
by Tony Blair, 1996

So Sally can't way
She knows it's too lay
She na na na naah

from 'Don't Look Back in Anger'
by Oasis, 1997

How my pen became a flower – but a flower I could write with

The great Phil Collins got it absolutely right. There truly *is* something in the air tonight. And it goes like this: buzzzzzzz. Yup, there's already an incredibly strong buzz around this book. Close friends and colleagues have been crying out for advance copies. The words 'stark', 'painful' and 'literally moving' are being bandied about by the people who matter.

It's a brave book, brave and intimate and intensely personal. It's a tale of rejection. Of sorrow. Of courage and fortitude in the face of almost insuperable odds. It's an unashamedly emotional tale of a woman who goes through this life armed only with an unselfish love of humanity and a transcendent humility. It involves a harrowing description of the tragic death of both my parents. And of my first husband in an untimely drowning accident.

My editor, Richard, bless him, was brilliantly right when he remarked over lunch that the passages concerning the death of these loved ones must have been almost unbearably hard for me to set down on paper. 'I know, I know . . .' I said, as a tear trickled down my left cheek, plip-plop-plipping with a poetry born of tragedy on to my Tuna and Aubergine Ciabatta Roll with Rocket Salad and New Potatoes. 'My creative powers were stretched to the full to imagine them all dead.'

There was a pause. 'They're not dead, Bel?' he said, ordering himself a large espresso. 'Your parents . . . your first husband – they're not actually dead?'

'Not strictly speaking, no,' I said, meditatively, 'not as such. But autobiography must be liberated from the strait-jacket of realism, don't you agree?'

'Your mother's anguished death from secondary smoking . . . your father's murder at the hands of a racist . . . and your first husband sacrificing himself for that washed-away border terrier off the pier at Great Yarmouth . . . it was confessional writing of the highest order,' Richard gasped. 'It must be true!'

'Thanks for that, Richard,' I said. 'But on the outmoded level of realism, my mum and dad are still living a typically bourgeois existence dividing their time between Cromer and a timeshare in Provence, and my first husband – damn him – is remarried to a South American and is currently working – or claims to be working – as a screenwriter in Los Angeles. But listen, Richard, I might have changed the odd detail, but the essence of the book is still horribly true. We're living in a confessional age, Richard. These things are just crying out to be told, however painful they may be to me as a person.'

'Do you mind if I ask you about that very painful incident when you were just 11 . . . and your Uncle Max . . . and the way he made you . . . and everything?' said Richard. 'Writing that must have taken one helluva lot of courage.'

'Yeah,' I sighed. 'The words just flooded out. And I didn't really have to change very much. I was really 20, not 11, and it was my first husband, not Uncle Max, and it was me doing it to him, not the other way round. But apart from that it's harrowingly close to what actually happened.'

You see, I strive to make my writing intensely personal, my God I do. My aim is to communicate the downs, the knocks, the hurts, the tears and the stark bloody tragedies of my own life for my readers to enjoy them at leisure.

2

Myself, I first began to write with this brand of searing personal honesty when I penned my now famous column, 'Littlejohn On Luv' in the *Observer*, in the early '70s. My best-loved piece was 'Vic's Vasectomy' (1973), a worm's-eye view of my second husband's operation. In loving detail, I showed how this one little snip affected his macho image of himself – in fact it affected him so badly that he was plagued by impotency for years after it was printed. But it turned Vic into something of a star, bless him – people would point at him in the street, smiling and then nodding sympathetically before looking away.

These pieces had begun with the momentous 'Only Three Days Into Our Honeymoon and Already He's Snoring Too Loud' (*Observer*, 7 June 1971). The rest, as they say, is history. It provoked an unprecedented response from readers, hundreds of them identifying with my pain, over two dozen urging me to 'Leave him, love'. If only I had taken their advice! But I battled on regardless, through thick and thin, thinking, I suppose, that I could save the guy from himself by embarrassing him each week in print.

The following week's article was equally up-front. 'For God's Sake Why Won't He Stop Leaving His Toe-Nail Clippings Over The Bathroom Floor?' first appeared in the *Observer* of 14 June 1971, though it has subsequently been anthologised many times. Over the next four years, I analysed, with at times painful honesty, the shortcomings of the man I had erroneously chosen as my husband. Memorable landmark pieces included 'Could Someone Please Inform Him About Personal Hygiene?' (*Observer*, 12 April 1972); 'The Day I Told Him What I Really Thought Of His Mum' (6 November 1973); and the award-winning 'Why Did That Insensitive Bastard Walk Out On Me?' (26 December 1974).

But like all men, he got his revenge, you bet he did. When he left me, he must have realised he was taking away my livelihood. After he walked out, I managed to squeeze per-haps half-a-dozen articles out of the new situation I found myself in – 'He Even Took The Hawkwind Triple Album' (*Observer*, 7 January 1975); 'Even If He Came Back, I'd Tell Him To Go Away' (*Observer*, 21 January 1975) etc., but before long the editor sent me a memo saying that unless my man returned pretty quick the series had run its natural course. My friends urged me to look around for another guy, preferably one worth writing about with searing honesty. They said it would inject more life into my column and gain me a bigger byline. The name Andrew Neil was even bandied about. But a woman's got her pride.

We divorced shortly afterwards ('Bel's Ta-Ra to Vic' *Observer*, April 1976) but have remained close through our lawyers ever since. And I still apply my offbeat sense of humour to writing about Vic with love and affection, ('The Funny Side Of Your Ex-Husband's Nervous Breakdown' *Observer*, August 1997).

With so little news around, personal honesty is an essential part of the columnist's armoury. When my son Marley was born in 1974, I wrote a memorable, deeply moving 2,000-word piece about his birth and the red-hot intensity of the love I felt for him. This piece got me to one helluva lot of award dinners. Luckily, I was able to attend them all as by that time Vic had custody of the kid. I received a record amount of reader comeback for my 'One Mum's Diary' sideways-look-at-life column in *The Times*, particularly for my pieces on Marley's terrible school reports ('Far From Satis' 8 July 1987), drink and drugs trouble ('My Baby's On The Bottle!' 28 Sept 1989) and subsequent expulsion from Summerhill ('Oo-er – He's Out!' 19 Feb 1990).

My parents have provided me with sufficient trauma for two highly praised volumes of autobiography. I covered my early suffering in the remorselessly honest *Daddy, I Knew You Too Well*, my seminal account of a childhood spent with a father who never managed to release himself from the uncontrollable urge to return home the moment he left work, and who would neurotically spend his entire weekends with us in our house, always desperate to please, even though he never really fitted into our play-structures. The opening line of that book – 'Damn you, Daddy, for never forgetting my birthday' – is now at the very heart of all the major works of literary quotation, not to mention countless theses at home and abroad.

My lovely, lovely publishers begged me for a follow-up. Their desperation paid off. My second work of auto-biography – *Mummy, I Was Irritated By Your High-Pitched Laugh*, subtitled 'and that common way you blew on your soup' – was an intensely personal, marvellously lyrical, occasionally painful, almost frighteningly truthful journey into the mother-daughter relationship. In what came to be regarded as perhaps its most hauntingly memorable scene I showed my one-eyed mother in grinding poverty, toothless and vengeful, her five-stone body shaking its last as she cursed me from her deathbed. For some, the launch party was marred by the arrival of a large, well-to-do woman with a high-pitched laugh bearing a large bouquet of flowers and calling herself 'Mummy'. It may or may not have been my mother, it's irrelevant, but only the most pedantic would argue that her *literal* survival detracts from the poetic truth – both searing and soaring – of that extraordinary deathbed scene.

Having written so poignantly of my father and mother, I am now contracted for a further two books, both describing journeys to hell and back. The first describes, with great dignity, my trials at the hands of my ex-husband (and Vic, if you're reading this, can I have my first edition of *The Golden Notebook* back and don't try and make out you don't know what I'm talking about because it's MINE and I can PROVE it because it's got MY name written in red felt-tip on the inside front cover, right?) and is due out next year. Pro-visionally titled *The Three-Glasses-of-Wine-a-Day Man*, it is the unflinching portrait of life with an alcoholic. Already, I've had excellent feedback from my publishers over the pivotal chapter in which I describe, in horrifying detail, the way my ex once spilt a glass of red wine over a white carpet –

and then (typical!) attempted to claim that I had nudged him with my left elbow whilst working out to *Rumours* by Fleetwood Mac. Talk about self-deception!

Painful honesty is not only the stuff of autobiography. With my well-known series of best-selling cookery books, the 'Coping With . . .' series, I have taken the trouble to inject the same intensely personal note. Sometimes I recall, just like Marcel Proust before me, but with more human warmth, the memories evoked by a particular dish. At other times, I try to let a note of my personal philosophy creep, undetected, into a recipe. And I am arguably at my best, as here, in my directions for my keynote recipe, Bel's Baked Eggs, when I combine the two:

I served this dish to the new man in my life just after my first divorce had come through. He was waiting in bed upstairs at the time – 'nuff said!

1) Heat the oven to Gas Mark 6 – but don't, for God's sake, put your head in it, as I was once driven to do by the sheer bloody money-grabbing self-centredness of my second husband.

2) Spread half the butter on the baking dishes in an even fashion, just as the wealth of the very rich should be redistributed to make for a kinder, more caring Britain.

3) Break in the eggs and sprinkle with salt. This always reminds me of my older sister Hannah breaking eggs on my head and throwing salt in my eyes when we were little. Hannah is now married to an alcoholic potter and living in a negative-equity house in a particularly dull part of Crawley.

4) Bake in the oven until the whites are milky, like my dear old grandma's eyes after the cataract took a grip. Enjoy!

Then there are my much-loved children's books. The lovely Marina Warner was among the first to notice that my 'Fluffy the Dolphin' series is also stamped through with my own character – idiosyncratic, passionate, caring, out-spoken, paradoxical, self-effacing and endearingly enig-matic. But even Marina failed to spot that large sections of it are entirely autobiographical, albeit transferred to the ocean floor. In *Fluffy the Dolphin and the Nervous Wreck* for instance, Larry Lobster is based upon my second husband. Sadly, Larry is boiled alive by a passing fisherman, Mr Happy. Similarly, the flirtatious Sophie Sea-Urchin is very loosely based on my fellow children's author Sophie Sanderson, who, much to everyone's astonishment, won the Whitbread Children's Book award last year, and good for her, she needed it, poor love. In my book, Sophie Sea-Urchin is alas crushed to death by Olly Octopus's tentacles on page two. It's the world we live in, nothing more, nothing less.

Needless to say, close friends tell me that my trouble is that I'm just too bloody honest. Hell, I can live with that. It goes with the territory. Let other columnists be 'witty', 'ironic' or 'intelligent'. I'm a writer. It's my job to tell it like it is. Readers, lovely readers, write in by their hundreds to congratulate me on my searing honesty. 'Your honesty is so searing,' one of them wrote last week, 'it's made me want mine seared too. What method do you recommend?'

Another question they ask is, 'What's the best routine for getting yourself going in this whole great writing thing every day?' Tricky one, this. Shame to say, there's no secret formula – sorree! Some writers have superstitious rituals to get them started, but I can't be doing with any of that non-sense. I prefer a more straightforward approach. In many ways, I am like George Eliot and Mrs Gaskell: before I sit down to write my articles, I always make a point of donning my leotard and working out on my exercise bike for between five and ten minutes. I then drink one glass of kiwi-fruit extract through a red-and-white striped straw, I slide a seventeen-year-old green-and-blue spotted handkerchief back and forth through the gap between my second and third fingers on my right hand for exactly two-and-a-half minutes, and then I sit down on my special writing chair, taking care to ensure that my left buttock always touches the cushion first. A simple enough routine, you'd have thought – but it always seems to do the trick.

One helluva lot of women – men too – have followed the brave lead set by me when I began my widely acclaimed 'Another Week Of Misery' column in the *Observer* four years back. Good luck to them – or rather bad luck to them, because a fair dose of bad luck is vital if you want to keep your column relevant.

I'll tell you how it began. In April 1993, I was asked to write a piece for the *Observer*. It was to be called 'The Pleasures Of Spring': daffodils, sunshine, frolicking lambs, chirruping birdies, the earth renewed, all that crap. The weekend before I was due to deliver it, my then partner, Geoff, announced that he had to – and I quote – 'get my karma sorted out by unscrewing my head and really wrapping it round some heavy thinking as to where it's at and where I'm at'. Geoff is a high-ranking management consultant with McKinsey, so he had to fit this process into the only available window of a single weekend.

Some kind of pleasurable spring that turned out to be. My piece wrote itself, it was that honest. Through a specially formulated program on my PC, I wrote the first word of each paragraph – 'I'. I then compiled a check-list of all the things that leapt roughshod into my mind at the mention of the word *spring*:

1) Just six months until winter.
2) Lambs to the slaughterhouse.
3) Poisonous snakes and vermin come out of hibernation.
4) Only 18 months until the winter after next.
5) Daisy chains can be fatal if they get stuck in the throat. Call for legislation?
6) Men – you can't trust them in spring.
7) Nor at any other time of the year for that matter.
8) They leave you on a Friday evening – the day they promised to put up the shelves, take the rubbish to the dump,

do something about the garden, clear up the garage, lose weight, ring up your mum with an apology, pull up their socks, cut down on their drinking, defrost the fridge, damn well stop trying to paw you and sort out the accounts. And they don't even have the grace to tell you why.

I took it from there, my pain and misery pouring out on to the page for everyone to devour. Readers, sick to death of phoney columns written by equally phoney columnists with even more phoney names, took to my confessional out-pourings like ducks to water. The editor, realising we were on to something, altered the title from 'The Pleasures Of Spring' to the more reader-friendly 'Another Week of Misery' – and the letters have never stopped flooding in.

The column soon became the stuff of legend. I wrote a thousand words every weekend about whatever had made me most miserable during the previous seven days. I stead-fastly refused to resort to the slick professionalism of the 'well-turned phrase', the 'cogent argument' or the 'keen observation'. These were not games I wished to play. One week, I would write about queuing at the 'fewer than six items' till in Sainsburys only to discover the person in front of me had eight items or above. The next, I would write about how a step-ladder I had bought from the local garden centre was impossible to dismantle – possibly a metaphor for my marriage. And the week after that I would try to com-municate that I was bored, unhappy, fed up, blah, blah – using all my powers as a writer to make the reader feel the same.

These days, Geoff is out of the picture (you're welcome to him, love!) but I still aim to start my pieces with searingly honest details about my day-to-day life, just to draw the reader in. Recent first sentences have begun, 'What was I doing, making myself a cup of instant coffee at 11.00 when I usually wait until 11.30?'; 'Could someone out there please tell me where I can find a salad-strainer that actually works?'; and 'Sometimes, I look at the keyboard, and I can't think of a thing to write'. In fact I'm developing this last one into a series.

I'm often asked what I do if I have nothing to write about. Easy. I give events a friendly nudge in the right direction. For instance, a piece which drew the most enthusiastic reader feedback ('anguished' raved one, 'desperate' another) was my seminal 'The Tears I Wept Upon Drowning The Kittens'. Until that morning I hadn't even thought of what I was going to write about. But I looked at my blank screen, then I looked at the clock ticking its way to the deadline, then I looked at those kittens, then at the bucket in the corner of the room, then back at the blank screen. After a brief struggle and a bit of splashing, a thousand compassionate words came flooding out. Magic!

Around this time I noticed a new niche in the newspaper market. Every week, more and more columns were devoted to the ailments of the most popular columnists. One of them, 'Me and My Verucca', by *Independent* columnist Joy Greenley, had even been nominated for a UK Press Gazette award. Another, 'Living With A Sore Elbow' by Wallace Arnold in *The Times*, was in its third year, and was greatly admired for attracting much-needed advertising revenue from the anti-sore-elbow drug companies.

First stop, my doctor, for an all-over check-up. The results? Disappointing: not much the matter. But he did say that I might just have the beginnings of an ulcer. And to guarantee a good night's sleep, I should take a little bit more care of my drink intake.

There was no time to waste. Before the end of the day, I was on to the editors of the health pages of four different national newspapers. And the rest is history. My major column, 'Coping with an Ulcer', ran in the Serious Illness and Weekend Motoring section of the *Sunday Times* for nearly two years, gaining a major trophy (The Wellcome Institute Ulcer Journalist Of The Year Award, 1990) in its first six months.

When my editor told me he thought my 'Coping With An Ulcer' column had run its natural course, I remembered my doctor's warning about alcohol. Was it possible that I – Bel Littlejohn – might be turning into an alcoholic? The idea was a nightmare. And, like all nightmares, worth at least 750–800 words.

A fortnight later, 'To Hell And Back With Bel Littlejohn', my devastating series of searingly honest insights was under way. Each week, I detailed, with chilling – and sometimes darkly comical! – honesty my descent into a nether world where one schooner of medium-dry sherry before dinner is simply not enough. Barely an evening went by without me also scrambling to the fridge and plunging headlong into a glass of dry white wine. My advice to my fellow women writers? Forget men. An illness is worth a thousand words.

But sometimes even an illness is not enough.

'I've brought you some flowers for your deathbed, Mama,' I said, my voice choking with raw and unfettered emotion. 'Take them, Mama, as a symbol of my big-hearted forgiveness for the very real hurt you've caused me throughout this life of mine – if you can call it a life.'

I leant forward to grab her gnarled old hand, the hand which, when I was aged just five-and-a-half, had denied me that second bowl of cornflakes just because I was – and the words echo like an unstoppable howl down the years – 'late for school'. For the first time, my mother spoke, the words tumbling out like so many mad doves from a cage, only without feathers on them.

'What do you mean – *deathbed*?' she said. 'I'm fit as a flea. Now, if you'll just pass me my cap, I've got a round of golf to play with Deirdre. By all means caddy if you like, dear.'

I sighed a mournful sigh. It had ever been thus: she had always denied me everything, and now, with savage predictability, she was denying me an emotional deathbed scene.

'But can't you *understand*?' I screamed, lovingly barring Mother's path to her golf-clubs by the front door. 'Can't you ever understand that I've just signed a generous contract to write a lyrical, haunting, harrowing yet beautifully honed account of my by turns painful, anguished and yet ultimately unresolved relationship with you? It's meant to culminate in a deathbed scene of transcendent forgiveness from me and agonised whimper of contrition from you – *and all you can say is that you're off to play golf!'*

'Let's sit down for a nice cup of tea and discuss things, Bel, love,' she said, once again rushing headlong into a state of denial about everything that had passed between us.

'But, Mama,' I sobbed, in a manner reminiscent of Plath at her most heartfelt and savagely caring, 'I have driven three-quarters of an hour, I have experienced an immense amount of trouble finding a parking meter, I have been specially to WH Smith for new fibre-tip pen and notebook, neither of them cheap – I have taken all that trouble and now you are saying that a deathbed scene is out of the question. Can't you ever think of anyone else for a change? What are my publishers going to say? Eh? Eh? Oh, Mother, Mother, Mother – why must you always *frustrate me so*?'

It was ever thus. One of my earliest memories – described in my book in clipped, raw sentences, adding up to a portrait of life in nappies that is at once plangent, poignant and pungent, overflowing with deep-seated feelings – is of my mother forbidding me, in that heartless way she never quite shed, to break a cut-glass in my brother's face. That was it. She was always more interested in possessions – her home and its contents – than in her daughter. Later on, in my miserable schooldays in an unforgivably luxurious private day-school (but a day-school that *would have been a boarding-school*, emotionally stultifying and soulless, had they run to the necessary dormitory facilities), many was the time I came back with a lovely new poem in my hands, which my mother, for all her cooing, would then refuse to have set to music and performed in the town hall by a fifty-strong choir and full orchestra.

No, no, no, no, no, no, no, no, no, no! My childhood echoed with refusals. No! Even though the other girls were always bringing something interesting to school, I was never allowed to saw the ears off my gymkhana pony and lovingly turn them into imaginative bookmarks. No! I was forbidden to enter the swimming-pool with my brother until I had – oh, stultifying, post-war petit-bourgeois mores! – removed the weights from his ankles. No! No matter how much I sobbed in bitter anguish, my mother would still never let me eat just one little goldfish from a tank that was full of them.

In the cold light of day, it's impossible to ascertain the full effect on my adult self of this devastating catalogue of childhood denial. Thanks to my mother's intransigence over the goldfish, in later life I've experienced tremendous difficulty in forming relationships of a lasting nature. For instance, I have lost count of the number of times I have compared my male partners to those goldfish I never had, growing endlessly frustrated at their total inability to open and shut their mouths without saying anything.

I suppose psychotherapists would call it some sort of gill complex, but for me the whole bloody thing is inextricably bound up with my very real sense of anger and frustration at my mother's emotional coldness. Why did she never react with anything but a soft smile when I punched her with oh so much love deep in her stomach? And now, 40-odd years on, why is she denying me the chance to sit at a desk writing – silently, wistfully, forgivingly – within spitting distance of her deathbed? With no dampening of her spite, she proudly claims the doctor says she could live to be a hundred. But there's such a thing as deadlines. What about my book, Mama – *what about my book*?

What is needed is a complete change of heart, and not just from my mother. Let's all vow to enter the New Millennium aspiring to that specific type of truth that transcends mere honesty. This book is intended to be nothing more nor less than a blueprint for the future. Fact is the new fiction. Searing, deeply upsetting confessionals from prominent authors like BL are the very stuff of the new literature.

With a couple of deaths in the family, a harrowing insight into the effect of divorce on a lonely child, and some vivid, fearless descriptions of masturbation, this major new work is assured a wide, intensely sympathetic readership. Readers are sick of the fictitious, the made-up, the fabricated. They're yearning for what's real, what's stark, what's almost unbearably sad. The conception may have been painful but, nine months on, my naked, painful, heartfelt reminiscences sit kicking and screaming in your hands.

Enjoy!

A is for Anger

i want to die now, alone and mouldy, hating everyone, always and forever

Like many of my fellow artists in the current 'Sensation' exhibition at the Royal Academy, I have a bleak vision of the world and my place in it. Crucify me if you want, but that's the way it is. In fact, I've had a bleak vision since I was just 12 years of age. The day my mother forced me to Dollond and Aitchison remains scorched upon my mind and my spectacles date from that time. And that's why the name of Littlejohn now means just one thing in the international artworld: bleak spectacles.

Just how bleak is for the viewer to judge. Like many of my generation, I began by thoughtlessly obeying the outdated norms of a previous era, painting watercolours of 'pretty' landscapes, flowers, buildings, blah, blah, blah. 'Cotswold Village in Spring', 'Lake Windermere at Twilight', 'A Host of Golden Daffodils', 'Sun Rising Over Exmoor': I was getting nowhere, and fast. But it all changed when a friend said it was about time I started looking at the world through my bleak spectacles. In one frantic fortnight, locked away in an Edmonton basement, I reworked all my earlier stuff. Just two months later the press were flocking to my mould-breaking exhibition, 'Skid Marks on Clean Linen' at the Saatchi Gallery. Tremendous excitement was whipped up by four of my works in particular. These were: 'Fresh Turd in Cotswold Village in Spring', 'Lake Windermere at Twilight: Child Drowning', 'Dead Daffs in Cracked Vase: Homage to Denis Nilsen' and 'Castrated Prick Rising Over Exmoor'.

Time Out described the Skid Marks show as 'complex and bleak', the *Guardian* called it 'genuinely bleak and uncompromisingly painful' and the *Sunday Times* gave it a rave, calling it not only 'bleakly resonant' but also 'resonantly bleak'. My art, my soul, my art-soul, had gained its identity: I was set on a lifelong course of isolation and bleakness, in which my bleak, isolated vision would be celebrated in some of the most happening galleries in London and I would find myself fêted on a scale I could previously have only dreamt of. And when my 'consistently bleak and numinously angry' (*Independent*) exhibition 'I Want to Die Now, Alone and Mouldy, Hating Everyone, Always and For ever' won me a place on the 1993 Turner Prize shortlist, I was totally over the moon, my prices shot up overnight, Charles Saatchi invited me and my partner to a private dinner with Richard Rogers, and, high on champagne and popularity, I felt I could live for ever.

Since then, I have been expanding away from the dead forms of traditional art – paints, canvas, brushes – into the more alive and happening 'Mixed media'. My 1994 exhibition 'Deck-Chair, Death-Chair' at the Serpentine Gallery developed my obsession with the form and structure of the deck-chair – coffin-like, spider-like, gallows-like, both tortuous and torturous – as a portent of death. My exhibit 'Fresh Turd in a Deck-Chair' twinned this obsession with an earlier obsession so effectively that Sarah Kent in *Time Out* was moved to describe the completed work of art as 'stark, raw, pungent, bleak and unsettling', the first time in the magazine's history that all five of those superlatives had been used simultaneously in the same sentence. Other exhibits included the now notorious 'Where are You God Now I Need You', consisting of a headless embryo in a deck-chair (now on tour in the Netherlands), and 'It's My Life or Would Be if it Was Which it isn't Much Really (Not Now, Not Ever)', an installation in which a putrid conger eel is threaded through the seat of a red-and-white striped deck-chair, which went on to win the 1994 Barbican Art Prize for the Longest Title in a Recent Exhibition.

And so to the 'Sensation' exhibition. I was going to enter a selection of my deck-chair installations when I heard on the art grapevine that Marcus was showing his Myra, and Chris was showing his Virgin Mary, and Marc was showing his head stewed in blood, and the Chapmans were showing their mutant pubescents. I knew straight away that a major re-think was needed if my work was to attract the kind of attention it deserved.

It was only a couple of weeks ago that I had my idea for my 'Death of a Princess' installations. 'Smashing Work' shows the torn-up body of a Mercedes Benz splattered with real blood. 'One for the Road' is a lifesize fibreglass model of a chauffeur, his hat askew, an empty bottle of French wine in each hand. When visitors pull a string on his back, he sings, bleakly, 'Down at the Old Bull and Bush'. The final installation, titled starkly 'Goner' – shocking maybe, but then death *is* shocking – has the naked Princess in an oxygen mask, and beside her a surgeon giving a stark, despairing thumbs-down sign. And no, 'Death of a Princess' is not prurient, immoral or distasteful. Art can be none of those things. In fact, it's a complex, concerned, sometimes teasingly ambivalent but always thought-provoking statement about death and illusion, about the friction between vulnerability and loss in the age of mass media. But above all, it's uncompromisingly *bleak*.

See it.

B is for Broken-Hearted

i just had to go and fall in love with him

I've made it a lifelong rule never to speak about my first husband, now a senior Labour cabinet minister, and I'm very sorry, guys, but I've no intention of breaking that rule now. Don't you think I've suffered enough? It was thirty years ago, and I've just about managed to put those dark days behind me. So please don't expect any vengeful revelations in this column about the little red squirrel whose amorous activities drove me to hell and back.

When I was approached by Linda McDougall to contribute an interview to her *Westminster Women*, I wanted to know whether her book was authorised. She told me it was entirely unauthorised, so I told her there was no way I would contribute less than four full-length interviews. I made it clear I had no wish whatsoever to rake over old grievances, that the mixture of infidelity, arrogance and cruelty that my ex had visited upon me during our brief marriage should not be used against him now, and that I would demand his total anonymity within her pages. Any physical description should be kept to a bare minimum (red hair, horrid beard, mad bulging eyes, over-blown sense of own importance, aggressive little stoat in bed and out) and the man in question would only ever be referred to by the code-name 'Roger Pook, Secretary of State for Abroad'.

With these provisos – the last thing I want is to wreck his career, or to draw attention to his gross unsuitability for high office – I granted Linda barely a dozen full-length interviews over a six-month period.

I told her I first met Roger Pook on an Arbroath dance-floor in 1969. In those days, he was no more than a feisty local councillor, but already one could detect tell-tale signs of a ruthless ambition at play. These were the early days of flower power, and many of his fellow males had arrived with flowers in their hair and garlands of inexpensive seasonal blooms around their necks. But Pook was determined to outshine them all. Early in the evening he had journeyed up and down the dance-floor, furtively distributing weed-killer from a watering-can on to the surrounding male foliage. Within ten minutes, he was the only guy in the hall with flowers still in his hair. And so, dammit, I just had to go and fall in love with him, didn't I?

When Roger Pook asked me to dance I found myself unable to say no. He had just offered me a chewy Dundee toffee. 'In the Year 2525' by Zager and Evans was playing on the turntable. Shouting over the music whilst flapping his arms to and fro, he detailed all the ways Zager and Evans had got it wrong. 'For all their undoubted tunefulness,' he yelled, 'these two don't seem to realise that by the year in question an ethical foreign policy combined with a reformed welfare state will make ample provision for the truly needy whilst preserving our position as a major player on the world stage.' Still in my teens, I was carried away by such rhetoric. And when he started elaborating on his schemes for a reorganisation of the state pension whilst we boogied on down to the Stones, I knew I was smitten. Within a fortnight we were honeymooning at Kirkcaldy, very handy, as Roger Pook enthused, for the Kirkcaldy race-track.

Yup, the old story is true. For Pook, the exercise of power was a powerful aphrodisiac. Even in those early days when he was only Vice-Chair of the Town Parking Committee, he would arrive back from a council meeting, having just forced through a motion entailing over fifty yards of double yellow lines in a built-up area near the town centre, his top-pocket laden with condoms.

Within the local Labour Party, he established a reputation for ethics second to none. The moment he was elected council leader, he made Arbroath a nuclear-free zone and issued a proclamation banning President Lyndon Johnson from entering the Arbroath council chamber until he had called an end to the Vietnam War. When the war did indeed end just a few short years later, Roger Pook pushed through a motion congratulating the Arbroath council for its role in bringing an end to a decade of senseless violence.

But outside the council chamber, Pook proved a very different character. It was while standing in the rain at the No. 3 bus-stop in Arbroath High Street, ready to embark on an important VIP fact-finding mission around the Gallashiels Town Sewage works, that Roger Pook, now a parliamentary candidate, announced, coldly and brutally, that I was not to accompany him. He would instead be taking his longstanding secretary, Miss Dolly McNaughtie, who, he informed me, had excellent shorthand skills and better understood the pressure on a public figure. As that No. 3 bus set off with the two of them in it, slooshing me with rain from a nearby puddle, I vowed there and then never to go public with my revelations of life with the Rt. Hon. Roger Pook, the cocky little runt. And I never have.

C is for the Child Within

hey! teecha! leave those kids alone!

The Floyd. Pink Floyd. The Pinks. Call them what you will, they've provided a lasting philosophical legacy for those of my generation who have spent their lives in fierce pursuit of truth, liberation and whatever.

Their songs have formed the soundtrack of our lives. *Ummagumma. Atom Heart Mother. The Piper at the Gates of Dawn. Bronze Eagle Defies the Planets. Winged Messenger from Oblivion. Dark Side of the Moon.* Albums like these, full of dense, often obscure, always haunting imagery helped to form the way we thought about life, and people, and what we really think we mean when we say we mean what we really think, or whatever.

'Money, It's a Crime' off *Dark Side of the Moon* album (1973) formed the basis of my political thought for the rest of the decade. It was a deserved success for the Floyd, who I now counted among my dearest friends. Dave Gilmour bought himself a beautiful Sussex mansion and a magnificent yacht, 'Piper at the Gates of Kash', with the proceeds, while Roger Waters, in typically broody, melancholic, fashion – let's never forget the guy's a genius – invested it in the gilt edge market, tripling the value of his investment portfolio in just over seven years.

But their greatest achievement was yet to come. In 1979, the Floyd released their most intensely political album yet. *The Wall* constituted a fierce indictment of everything that had gone before them; as such it was an instant success, soaring to number one in the charts, earning them over £300 million in the next four fiscal years, and buying both Roger and Dave the freedom from possessions and consumer durables they had craved for so long.

The most celebrated song off that historic album was surely 'Another Brick in the Wall', a defiant attack on traditional methods of schooling, with its searing chorus, 'We don't need no educashun! . . . Hey! Teecha! Leave Those Kids Alone!' It proved a watershed in my life. That year my then-husband Vic and I had been searching in vain for a suitable school for our son Marley. We have been looking for a learning environment where Marley's many undoubted talents – for forceful, non-verbal argument, for wine-tasting, for paper-tearing and animal surgery – could be channelled to his best advantage. As luck would have it, we were driving through the back lanes of Suffolk in our 2CV when that momentous Floyd track came on the radio. 'Next left, Vic!' I screamed, 'Summerhill Heer We Kum!'

As you know, Summerhill was founded by the Scottish visionary A.S. Neill, who once summed up his educational philosophy in the sentence, 'I would rather produce a happy street-sweeper than a neurotic prime minister.' Of course, the guy couldn't achieve this dream every single time, but the Old Alumni section of the school mag usually carries the latest news from a varied selection of neurotic street-sweepers. But at least he realised an essential truth of human life: we have more to learn from kids than they have to learn from us.

To use a qualitative judgement the founder would rightly despise, Marley did well at Summerhill. Within a year, he had killed and partially cooked two pigeons, he had played a vital part in a democratic school tribunal that had passed a suspended life sentence on a serial offender, who had twice in one week called the English teacher by her surname, he had wiped his fellow actors off the stage in the title role of the school play *Lord of the Flies*, and he had sailed through his end-of-year exams, most of the time on a friend's boat moored at nearby Walberswick.

And now what? Your average blinkered inspectors from the Department of Education are threatening to close down the school, just because most of the kids don't meet their own Thatcherite standards of 'education'. Okay, so maybe they can't read and write – but when's that ever been the point of school? Last year, two of those so-called 'uneducated' kids achieved a Grade C in Mime and Woodwork, another two gained their Cycling Proficiency badges, Grade B, thank you very much, and an under-matron gained her black belt in karate. A senior pupil successfully completed an original nature poem inspired by William Wordsworth, 'Daferdills', and the school budgerigar, Tarantino, won the underwater swimming competition, for which he was awarded a posthumous trophy.

As the headteacher of Summerhill said in a recent interview, 'It's this Labour Government that has a lot to learn from Summerhill, not vice versa.' Perhaps if Gordon Brown was less uptight about whether or not to join the EMU, he would smile a bit more – after all, what's the point of being Chancellor of the Exchequer if you can't hang loose once in a while? If only Mr and Mrs Brown had sent Gordon to Summerhill, there might have been far less of the hangdog, don't-interrupt-while-I'm-doing-my-sums expression. It all comes back to The Floyd. They once said – and I quote – 'When the Kraken Slams the Door, the Piper Leaves the Mansion'. And that's a phrase only a Summerhill kid could ever truly understand.

C is also for Choked

a candle in the wind

[1]

I wrote this powerful, award-winning piece straight after watching Diana, Princess of Wales being interviewed on the Panorama *programme. I was, I think, the first to discover that Diana was not just a woman: she was ALL women. This was later to become a key text in my Diana Studies course at the University of Oxbridge.*

She's hurting dreadfully, poor love. And she doesn't care who knows it. They may dismiss her as weak, but there's strength in her weakness. And, what's more, there's weakness in her strength.

Snap!

I too have trod this path. This path too I have trod. And in trodding this path, I too have grown, I too have expanded, S to XL within the hour, and back again an hour later once the fridge door slammed shut. Welcome to the sisterhood, Diana. Sit back and enjoy the ride.

Lady Diana Spencer was born with a silver spoon in her mouth. But it never quite fitted. Sometimes the handle got caught beneath her tongue. Sometimes the spoony bit made the roof of her mouth feel a bit awkward. But, my God, she stuck it out, and now she's extracted the damn spoon and is hitting the Establishment over the head with it in a proud gesture of feminist defiance.

She was still a schoolgirl when she first met her Prince so-called Charming. Welcome to the fairytale, love. Only he turned out not to be Prince Charming at all. He turned out to be a wolf. A wolf dressed in her grandmother's clothes. Could someone please tell me what the Prince of Wales was doing dressing up in an outfit belonging to The Honourable Ruth, Lady Fermoy? Welcome to the Male Establishment, where such practices are all in a day's work.

Trapped in a loveless marriage, Diana began to look in on herself. She felt locked in by the Establishment. Every morning when she woke up in bed next to her husband, there was the Honourable Nicholas Soames lying beside them, stuffing his face with breakfast sausages, monitoring her every movement and reporting it back to his paymasters in MI5.

It can't have been much of a life. A life it can't much have been. In the words of the song:

In the summertime, when the weather is fine
Gonna la la la la la la la la wine

Only the weather wasn't fine, and there was precious little wine left in the purse.

As the years went by, she realised she could reach out her arm right over the heads of the British Establishment, way past the fat male bellies of the Old Boys in White's, through the Dartford Tunnel, all the way across the English Channel to the Continent, and from there right across oceans until finally she could find herself holding the hands of those who were truly in need. Meanwhile, she would keep her other arm close to her in her cage in Kensington Palace, ready with a Royal hankie to wipe her own tears away.

Diana's dilemma was – is – the dilemma of women the world over. Through this Bosnia-style conflict within her own family, she has proved herself a nineties' woman with nineties' concerns. There are a lot of us out there, love. With that long arm of hers, she has reached for the mirror on the other side of the room and taken a long, hard look. And what she sees in that mirror is her own face staring back. In the words of the song:

'Doo wah diddy diddy dum diddy do'

Only in her case the *doo wah* has no *diddy diddy*, and the *dum diddy* didn't. Did he or didn't he? Diana doesn't give a *doo wah*. And she's certainly not *dum*.

On television the other night, she came across as a woman just like me, a woman shaking it up and shaking it down but never quite shaking it off, a woman who is, above all, a mother to all she meets. A mother to you, a mother to me. A mother to her children, a mother to her parents. A mother to the Queen Mother. The Queen Mother Mother: that's a role Di could perform with incredible strength, a caring, international role for a girl who, in the space of twenty years, has grown into a woman.

We have all of us been through what Diana's been through. My second husband was just like Prince Charles – the blue jackets, the 'concern', the male and female friends. And even though he wasn't a Prince of the Realm working out of Kensington Palace but a Systems Analyst working out of Leamington Spa, he displayed many of the passive-aggressive male characteristics that Diana found in Charles. For reasons I won't go into – my husband was a control freak – I was unable to invite the *Panorama* team into my house to hear my side of the story. But if I had been able to, I would have said just about almost exactly what the Princess said. Like Diana, I too want to be the Queen of Hearts, cutting the heads off those who seek to steal my tarts.

We are both strong women, Di and I, women who magnificently, defiantly – but not without blood, sweat and fears – have learnt to face the world head-on, to reclaim a private life for ourselves and our children by repeating word for word before a forgiving viewing public some of the most intensely personal conversations we ever had.

Knowledge, as Di said, is power. But how do you spell knowledge? With a 'd' or without? From now on, Diana can spell it any way she damn well wants. As the song says:

Da doo ron ron ron da doo ron ron.

Only for true feminists, believe me, this particular Di can *doo* no *ron*.

[2]

A hectic, hectic, hectic week, with the media asking me over and over again to comment, comment, comment. As I said in a pre-recording for *The World at One* in my fifth interview of the morning on Tuesday, 'Frankly, I'm drained. Everything that might be said has already been said. I'm in a state of numbness, a state of shock. I appeal for a time of silence, a time for private grief. There's nothing more to be said.'

'Smashing!' chipped in the producer. 'But could you just say that once more, Bel, only instead of saying "There's nothing more to be said", could you say "There's obviously far more to be said on this dreadful tragedy in the days and weeks to come". Then we can segue it in with all the other comments. Smashing!'

So we recorded it again, just in time for me to go straight through to the *Woman's Hour* studio to discuss the tragedy from a deconstructionist feminist angle with Bea Campbell, Jo Brand and Edwina Currie. Then a ten-minute break before being whisked off to Radio 5 Live with David Mellor, to discuss, from a mother's angle, with Clare Rayner and

Bernard Ingham, what thoughts must be going through the young Princes' heads at this tragic time. As a professional broadcaster, I feel it my duty to offer views on matters of national importance even if, at times like these, I would rather confront my grief in a more intensely personal manner.

As I wrote in a moving piece in the *Guardian* the day after she passed over, I'll never forget where I was when I first heard the news. Like chalk on a blackboard, it'll never be erased from my mind: I was in my home, listening to the radio or watching the television, either in the kitchen or in the bedroom, when I heard Jim Naughtie – or was it Martyn Lewis? – delivering the fateful news.

Before long, the telephone began to ring and ring and ring. I had to fall back on my experience of nearly thirty years as a professional journalist and broadcaster. I took a deep breath and willed myself to overcome my personal emotions for the greater public good: for the nation, I simply had to comment.

I can be pretty certain I was the first professional commentator that morning to employ the word 'icon'. It was while being asked my thoughts on the tragedy by Dave Lee Travis on Peterborough Sound. 'Above all,' I said, 'she will be remembered as an icon.'

Travis was visibly moved. 'An icon . . .' he repeated thoughtfully, '. . . and we'll be hearing more from Bel Littlejohn on this untimely tragedy after this, from Kajagoogoo.'

It wasn't long before the rest of the media latched on to my word, begging me to repeat it and expand on it. To Trevor McDonald, I described her as 'an icon of the modern age', to Sue Macgregor as 'a feminist icon', to Richard and Judy as 'an icon of the television age', to Anna Raeburn on Capital Radio as 'an icon of betrayed womanhood', to David Dimbleby as 'an icon of the 20th century' and to Jimmy Young as 'an enduring icon of caring and compassion'.

At the end of the week, the *Observer* will be carrying Bel

Littlejohn's 'The Princess the Public Never Knew: a Personal Reminiscence by One Close to Her'. It will offer my deeply moving analysis of the real woman behind the mask, the Princess who existed away from the spotlight, away from all the media razzamatazz, an icon, if you will, of privacy. And I'll be drawing heavily on my personal experience.

My qualifications are second to none. For a time, I was very, very close to the Princess. The time was 7.15 p.m. on 23 June 1992. With fewer than two hundred other people in that historic cinema foyer, I was able to gather a first-hand impression of the real Princess, the Princess who kept her real thoughts and emotions hidden from the Press at large. It's hard to express what I felt, but I saw her somehow as . . . as . . . as . . . an *icon* who seemed to know instinctively that she was who she was, and that what she was was what no one else was who was not what she was, and, *moreover*, that no one who was not what she was was able to know who or what she was as well as she was. This realisation hit me that night like a blow from a candle.

In the book I am now writing, *Diana and Bel: a Very Private Friendship*, I draw on this unique experience to explain what it was like to be completely alone in that room with the Princess and two hundred others. She was a meteor, a rocket trailing through the evening sky like a knife through honey, a sacrificial lamb who lit up all our lives by building bridges and gathering the morning dew, a spring flower, its petals touching so many lives at the first sniff of wind, a true icon for our times, Che Guevara in a Versace dress, Rupert Brooke in a tiara.

It is up to those of us blessed with the ability to create pictures in words to interpret the semiology of the Princess for our readers and our viewers. And for those of us in the business of commentary and overview, analysis and explanation, one word alone remains more vital than all the others: icon, icon, i-con.

She taught us what love is. She taught us how to laugh and how to cry. And the difference between the two. Crying's the one with tears, laughing's usually noisier. She gave us our freedom. She gave us a life-long lesson in releasing our emotions. She blew aside a thousand years of tradition and reached out her hand through the net curtain of our emotions to smooth our pain away. And, my God, she taught me how to write – not just with your fingers and thumbs, but by employing the best bits of your whole body. Yes, she taught me how to write with my nose.

She taught us how to eat, not just with a snooty, starchy knife and fork, dammit, but with whatever implements came to hand: a ballpoint pen, a cassette, a garden trowel. She held up a mirror to the nation, advised us on a suitable conditioner and helped us cope with split ends. Into our empty hearts, she poured the finest extra virgin olive oil, a little chopped-up garlic and some sun-dried tomatoes. And by doing so, she taught us how to make the perfect pasta. And she taught us as a nation how to shield ourselves from the weather. Elton put it just right in his memorable re-write of the powerful fifth verse of 'Candle in the Wind':

And it seems to me you lived your life
Like a Candle in the Wind, never
Going out like a sunset when the rain set in
Expecting light drizzle with sunny periods,
Keeping out the cold, but letting in some air, and
Waiting for the snow to fall when the rainbow came up.

It seems that every great writer has paid his or her respects to the memory of the Princess these past few days. Writing in the *Daily Mail*, Alexander Solzhenitsyn confirmed her as 'the caring Princess, who made us all happy and taught us to frolic'. In the *Independent*, Harold Pinter wrote one of his rare poems:

We miss you Di
And that's why we cry
With your lovely smile
As wide as a mile
You were our Candle in the Wind
And your memory will never be binned.

And in a moving tribute in the *Scotsman*, Irvine Welsh said 'Ma heid's feckin' nippin' this mornin', Diana, becos you wer oor fuckin' Quin of Herts.'

And let me tell you this. I was proud to be a member of the *Guardian* these past, desperately miserable ten days, when more word-processors were literally flooded with tears of grief than at any other time in this newspaper's great history. In our coverage, we recognised in our every word, our every phrase, this one great truth: it is not every day a human being dies. And when a human being dies who is not only rich and gorgeous and single, but, perhaps above all, royal and aristocratic – well, that is surely the time when all the other news in the world must be finally taught its place.

It was surely right that the death of the Princess dominated our hearts and our pages last week. All other world events were eclipsed by that tragic news – possibly the most tragic home news since the Black Death of 1346. But that's not to say we ignored it all. 'Tragedy as 500 Foreigners Die in Air Crash Before Hearing Latest on Diana' was one of our stories towards the bottom of page 25. Another story – 'China Declares War on West: Millions Perish' – almost made it into the third edition last Monday, but, unable to get any relevant photographs of Diana in Peking, we put it on hold.

Now, with the Nation in pieces, is the time to rebuild. I fully support the calls to re-title Heathrow Airport 'Diana, Princess of Wales Airport' – and who really cares that the time taken to say it will cause an estimated twelve per cent of passengers to miss their connections? But it should not end there. Kensington Gardens – that beautiful space in London which Diana planted, mowed and tended all by herself – must be urgently renamed Diana, Princess of Wales Gardens. The M25 must be renamed the M Diana, Princess of Wales 25, and the House of Commons must be re-called at once to push through plans to rename their historic bell-tower Big Diana. Trevor McDonald has already agreed, as a gesture of respect, to alter the main news broadcast on independent television to Princess at Ten.

And, after a word with Tony and Peter, I can confidently predict that at the forthcoming New Labour conference it will be announced that the party the Princess so loved, and felt so much a part of, will shortly be repositioning itself as New Dianalabour. At the same time, in a remarkable gesture towards the public mood Peter Mandelson and the board of trustees of the Millennium Experience will be announcing that the Dome will now be topped with a 200-yard long tiara, and the entire project renamed The Diana Millennium Experience.

Finally, I am proud to say that, as a gesture of respect to the memory of the most compassionate woman who ever lived, the editor of the *Guardian*, in consultation with the Scott Trust, has agreed to change the name of the newspaper to something more fitting, more in keeping with the public mood. And I for one will be proud to continue to write – caringly, compassionately – about matters of grave national importance for that great newspaper, the *Guardiana*.

D is for discipline

get down and get with it

Lay off him, guys: Alastair Campbell has done one helluva lot for the New Labour Movement, and it's high time we gave him a break. And that's official – recently those of us on the senior level of government advisers received a letter signed simply 'Yours sincerely, an Official Spokesman'. It said: 'It's high time you laid off Alastair Campbell and gave him a break' and 'If you do not, you can just P-I-S-S off, because you're just a load of C-R-A-P anyway, so who bloody cares.'

Alastair has always had a way with words. It's widely known that he first made his name as a wordsmith way back in the early 1970s, when he was the award-winning lyricist with the socially aware progressive rock group Slade, fronted by his longstanding colleague Dave Hill.

It's an open secret within New Labour that Alastair continues to pride himself on smuggling Slade lyrics into the speeches he writes for the Prime Minister, thus ensuring the support of millions of their former fans. 'My vision for Britain,' said Tony in a major pre-election speech in Halifax this time last year, 'is one of national renewal, a country with drive, purpose and energy, a country in which the dignity of each and every citizen is a right, not a privilege.

So let's get down and get with it and cum on feel the noize because, frankly, both nationally and internationally, mama, weer all crazee now.' The speech brought people of the '70s generation to their feet – yet surprisingly few of the professional commentators were able to detect the essential Campbell/Slade hallmarks that had subliminally triggered it.

But Alastair's forceful way with words has never, as some hard-left Tory commentators have implied, been employed to influence senior ministers in Tony's administration. Far from it. Once he's told them what to say, he stands well back from the spotlight and the microphone and just lets them get on with it. The other day, I was delighted to bump into Alastair at a purely routine dinner reception for Mr Murdoch at Number 10. (Incidentally, it's a sign of Tony's growing reputation that he has gained the confidence of such an experienced world-leader as Mr Murdoch, and it's high time we in New Labour gave him credit for it.)

Anyway, Alastair had gathered a select group of ministers to pay tribute to Mr Murdoch on an informal basis. Before Mr Murdoch's arrival, Alastair assembled them in his Downing Street office to offer them friendly encouragement. 'Is your hair hurting, by any chance?' he asked the lovely Chris Smith, as he stood in line.

'Not at all, sir,' replied Chris, smiling sweetly.

'Well, it bloody well oughter be because I'm standing on it, you 'orrible little man! Get it cut!' said Alastair.

'Thank you kindly, sir,' said Chris, with genuine gratitude, but by this time Alastair had moved down the line to Robin Cook.

''Ow's the bird, then?' asked Alastair.

'Bearing up very well under the circumstances, thank you for asking, sir!' replied Robin.

'Gonna make an honest woman of her, are we, then?' said Alastair.

'Yes, sir! With your permission, sir!' replied Robin.

''Cos we wouldn't want to upset Mr Murdoch, would we, now? And we wouldn't want to lose our lovely big house in

34

the country with its lush lawns and full complement of servants, would we now, eh?'

'No, sir! Honest woman, sir!'

No prizes for guessing that these off-the-record informal conversations will be caricatured in the Tory press as showing that Alastair has ideas above his station. Yet the ministers concerned were all very grateful for his advice, making their thanks clear in spontaneous written submissions, signed and countersigned in his presence, now available on request from the Downing Street Press Office.

And the reception went very smoothly, with each minister being presented by Alastair to Mr Murdoch, who was very good at putting them at their ease, sharing a joke or a political insight with them before sending them on their way with a pre-arranged signal.

Incidentally, it's Alastair who's had the vision to set up the Millennium Bug task-force. There have been growing fears in Government circles that at the stroke of midnight on 31 December 1999, Tony will revert to the year 1900, growing side-whiskers, donning a frock coat, deporting shoplifters and demanding a full policy review for the relief of Mafeking. And if the Bug proves difficult, it'd better watch out, 'cos it'll have Alastair to answer to, bless him.

E is for Empathy

ted and bel and sylvia

It takes a poet to understand a poet. And that's why people look to me for the key to Sylvia Plath.

No, I did not 'know' Sylvia in any pedantic, literal sense of the word. Strictly speaking, I never 'met' her, either before or after her demise. But in a far more interesting sense, I knew – and know – the real Sylvia probably better than any other human being alive on this strange and beautiful planet, this 'frozen blood-orange trapped in a juice-extractor', as I described it in one of my most searing and memorable poems. And I certainly know sylvia more intimately – of this much we can be sure – than Ted Hughes ever did.

I first grew close to Sylvia in the autumn of 1963, a few short months after she had passed away. Over lunch with my editor, Richard, it was suggested that he would be delighted to publish my own first volume of poetry, *Words Unwritten*, in a limited edition of between fifty and a hundred copies, depending on market demand, so long as I would deliver a definitive biography of Sylvia Plath for their spring catalogue. Richard had heard rumour on the grapevine, he said, not only that Plath had once been a friend of Lee Harvey Oswald, but that her estranged husband Ted

Hughes had regularly had Fidel Castro down to stay in his Devon farmhouse. Perhaps I could work it in.

It is widely acknowledged in academic and literary circles where I live that the resulting biography *Bel and Sylvia: a Literary Friendship* (1964) entered into the mind of Sylvia Plath as no other writer has ever done, before or since, not even Sylvia, who was inevitably divorced from a true understanding of herself by her proximity to the subject. It urged the reader to rediscover the poetry of Plath, not by the superficial act of going to a library or bookshop and reading all those words of hers but by the infinitely more *empathetic* method of making friends with Sylvia, putting her words to one side and immersing oneself in the minutiae of her childhood, her marriage, her tempestuous affairs.

Though I never managed to trace the direct link between Plath and Oswald or Hughes and Castro, I felt that the deeper symbolic truth was more important, so I included it. There is also a particularly vivid passage in *Bel and Sylvia* in which the biographer lays the blame for a number of other things – Sylvia's death, the male colonisation of her memory, the female crisis of confidence, the Suez Crisis, the decline of Britain as a post-war industrial power – fairly and squarely at the door of Ted Hughes.

My Plath biography soon became seminal at home and abroad, gaining me my Visiting Professorship at the University of Amarillo. During that time I enhanced my status as a leading academic, poet and biographer with the publication of a second, profoundly moving, long overdue study of Plath's daily life, *Up the Garden Plath: the Essential Sylvia*.

Needless to say, my researches met with a wall of silence from Hughes. To my simplest request – for Sylvia's exact waist measurements, for the name and address of the store from which she purchased her original bell jar, for information concerning her preferred mid-morning snack, for private photographs of the two of them on holiday together, for a brief signed confession from Hughes acknowledging blame for her death and begging forgiveness from those of us who knew and loved her – I met with a curt, typewritten letter of refusal. So much for artistic integrity . . .

And so we arrive at the publication of Ted Hughes's new book of poems about his relationship with sylvia Plath, written, I suspect, in some kind of vain attempt to prove that he somehow knows more about the two of them than all the serious writers and academics who have been labouring at the coalface of Plath Studies for the past thirty or more years. Judging from the factual inaccuracy of the poems I have read so far, they are of no value at all to future biographers. In one poem, for instance, Hughes contends that Sylvia wore a 'blue flannel suit' for her first class at college: can he really be so unaware of recent Plath scholarship not to realise that research has shown it was in fact far more likely to have been a blue *brushed cotton* suit? Some poem that turned out to be!

With this untimely publication, Ted Hughes has done the cause of poetry studies no good at all. Myself, I would like to return to Sylvia's verse, which must stand by itself in its purity, free from tittle-tattle. And that's an argument I'll be forcefully espousing in my forthcoming book, *Sylvia and Ted: Behind Closed Doors*. Buy it.

E is also for extracting experience

extracts from my new millennium dome experience diary

23 May 1997

Talk about hitting the ground running! It's been go, go, go ever since last week, when Peter (Mandelson) appointed me Youth Adviser to the Millennium Dome. 'We've got to get youth on our side, Bel – and you're the one who's going to do it for us!' he said. 'After all, wasn't it you who went to Woodstock?'

'No,' I explained, 'but I heard the album.'

At our inaugural meeting, Peter said our first task was to think of a better name than just boring old 'Dome'. 'We've got Cameron Mackintosh putting a brand new revival of *Jesus Christ Superstar* on the revolving stage, we've got Tom Jones as Jesus and Cilla Black as Mary Magdalen, we've got Richard Rogers's fabulous, very '50s-stroke-'60s design for the building itself. Now all we've got to do is think of a very up-to-the-minute, really happening name for the event. Any ideas, guys?'

'"The Millennium-a-go-go"?' suggested David Jacobs, who's overseeing the music side of things. 'In my day, that used to suggest something frightfully jazzy.'

'Nah!' chipped in Janet Street-Porter, Jacobs's deputy. 'Get a life, grandad! That's dead square, that is! We should call it "TFI Millennium" – or better still "DEF II Millennium" after my mould-breakin' show. Anyone see it? Fuckin' grooverama, it was.'

At the head of the table, Peter looked uncertain. 'Alan – any ideas?' he said, turning for advice to New Labour's specialist in future trends.

'Greetings, pop pickers!' replied leading DJ and trend-setter *par excellence* Alan Freeman. 'Howsabout the Millennium Roadshow – that's got a happening-type feel about it, dontcha think – not arf! All right, Pete, me old mate? Right! Stay bright! This is your old mate Fluff sayin' tara for now! Ta-ra!'

'Thanks for that valuable contribution, Alan,' concluded Peter, 'but I'm not sure we've quite cracked it yet. Over to you, Bel!'

'Thanx, Peter,' I said, 'you know, I went to a truly brill concert in Norwich last night, with all my fave bands on one bill – not just Hawkwind and The Groundhogs but Peter Green too, can you believe. And you know what they called it? "The Alternative Experience". And I think that's what we should call it if we want to be truly where it's at as Big Ben strikes midnight on 31 December 1999 – yup, "The Millennium Experience".'

Sure enough, Peter was over the bloody moon. 'That's the one!' he said. 'Yeah! The Millennium Experience! It's so *now*, it's so *happening*, it's so *totally good hair day*!'

I'd be lying if I said I wasn't dead chuffed to have my own title chosen. Sorry, Janet, love!

17 June 1997

'Were going to be asking all the big questions, Bel,' enthused the lovely Peter Mandelson. 'Who are we? What are we doing here? Where are we going? How are we getting there?'

'Would you like more Brie?' I asked.

'That too,' he said and continued, 'all the big questions

under one roof – that's the name of the Millennium game.'

It was then that he turned to me and looked me straight in the eye. 'And Bel,' he said, 'I want you also to be Chair of our Spirit Zone.'

I was totally knocked sideways. 'You've knocked me back-wards, Peter! It's like being hit from behind!' I gasped. But then a still, small voice began to speak to me, a voice I recognised at once as my spirit guide, Little Running Water.

'Your country is crying out for a high-profile multi-faith spiritual dimension Dome Zone to explore the relevance of faith in the 21st century within an ongoing cross-cultural environment, with provisional sponsorship from one of our leading household furnishing suppliers,' whispered the still, small voice. At that instant, I knew this was one job I simply had to do.

Is there a God? Well, *is* there? Over wide-ranging dis-cussions with Peter, we sought to thrash out a clear answer to this longstanding question. Basically, I took the line that there probably is some form of Higher Power, not a God in the old-fashioned, paternalistic sense but a kind of spiritual *thing* or *dimension* through which we might recognise some sort of unity or spiritual-type *thing*. Peter took an open stance, believing in a oneness about the universe that some-times makes you think there really is something out there, something beyond ourselves – after all, in an earlier life he was Rameses II, Pharaoh of Egypt, son of Seti I, builder of the great rock temples at Abu Simbel, precursors, in their primi-tive way, to the great New Millennium Dome. And the Dome will live in the minds and hearts of its subjects for as long as the Pyramids – or at the very least until it's taken down in a year or two.

28 July 1997

How should we convey the very real spiritual yearnings of the British people on the cusp of a new millennium within the overall framework of an interactive exhibition? For the moment, it's strictly top secret, but I'm hoping for teacup rides around a lifesize Garden of Gethsemane with real bunny-rabbits, a Mohammedobile catapulting you into the truly magical fairytale world of Islam, and a virtual reality Archbishop Carey transported around the Dome on a cloud at speeds of up to 350 mph. Believe me, if there is a God, he or she will be literally knocked backwards.

22 September 1997

All too predictably, politically motivated tabloid critics are claiming that we have nothing to put in the Dome. What nonsense! Our meeting today will have confounded all their doom and gloom.

'At this stage, I feel absolutely certain that we should have a theme . . .' announced Stephen Bayley, leaping up and down in his seat. His experience at the recent Coca-Cola exhibition fully justifies him in seeing himself not only as a Design Guru but also as a Can Guru. 'And I am convinced that the theme should begin with the letter T. You see, we've formulated a brilliant Tuscan-style logo with more than a hint of Gaudi plus a smidgen of Dada around the letter T, and it would be a desperate shame to waste it.'

'T . . . T . . . T . . .' I pondered. 'What about Tennis? People love tennis . . . I'm thinking racquets, I'm thinking Wimbledon, I'm thinking all white, I'm thinking strawberries and cream . . . and we could fit . . . what? – eighty or so tennis courts into the Dome.'

'Or Tortoises?' chipped in Cameron Mackintosh. 'After all, the Dome is just like the shell of a tortoise – and the live show could echo the theme. I see it now: Les Tortoises – the musical. Just like *Cats*, only less furry.'

'And Turtles – let's not forget they begin with a T, too!' said Michael Heseltine, still a powerhouse of ideas.

'And Trolleys!' declared Peter M. 'People love trolleys. Shopping trolleys, airport trolleys, the lot. And Tent Pegs. They begin with a T too, if I'm not mistaken. What about an exhibition of tent pegs of the future, eh? We'd pull in the outdoorsy types!'

Stephen tapped his Mont Blanc on the table. 'I've got it!' he said. 'T for Time!'

'Milk, two sugars, if you're offering,' said Michael Heseltine.

'I said "T for Time",' snapped Stephen. 'We could celebrate all types of time, each with its own section. Action Time. World Time. Culture Time. Junior Show Time. Tea Time. Once Upon a Time. Rag Time. Drive Time. Half Time. Time Gentlemen Please. At This Point in Time. Time Travel. Breakfast Time. Thoroughly Bad Time. Anyone got the Time. Time I Was Leaving.'

In an instant, we knew we had struck gold.

'For "Time Gentlemen Please" we could recreate the public house of the 21st century,' suggested Peter, 'all much the same as the 20th century, but with more lagers from Mexico.'

'And for "Junior Show Time" we could always try to get a signed photo of Bonnie Langford. She was very good, and a particular favourite of Tony's,' said Chris Smith. 'Incidentally, I wonder what Lena Zavaroni is doing these days?'

5 November 1997

We've already assembled half a dozen Mexican lagers, a signed photo of Bonnie Langford, the loan of an alarm clock (At This Point in Time), three catering packs of PG Tips (Tea Time), half a dozen freshly laid eggs (Breakfast Time) and the promise of a long white line from Dulux Emulsion (Half Time). A good 28 months left to go – and we're already halfway there! And the commercial sponsorship is rolling in, the loan of a second-hand moped from Honda (Drive Time) officially confirmed. So much for the scaremongering stories about so-called 'rifts' between Stephen and Peter put out by the hostile press! Stephen is an indispensable part of the team. The Millennium Experience will be up and running by 2003 at the latest. And the title of the new packaging concept? 'Extra Time.'

12 December 1997

Thank heavens Stephen Bayley has gone – about time too! Now we can all roll up our sleeves and really get down to work! I have spent an exhausting but creatively satisfying five days in a design studio in Clerkenwell dressed in a leotard, striking poses both caring and courageous, futuristic, yet grounded in the past. I was, of course, modelling for the central figure, two hundred and fifty feet tall, that's set to grace the Dome.

The Littlejohn, as the figure is affectionately termed, will welcome up to 10,000 paying customers parading inside her mind and body everyday. Peter M is hugely excited by my suggestion that the Mind Zone section of The Littlejohn should be decorated with holograms of my collected articles, thereby offering ordinary people a rare insight into the mind of the writer of today. He says he'll chew on it.

14 February 1998

Snipers, eat your hearts out! If there's one thing that gets on my wick – and Tony's wick too, bless it – it's the cynics and carpers who can think of nothing better to do with their lives but whinge on about the Millennium Experience while the rest of us roll up our sleeves and set about the uphill task of trying to spend £750 million.

But today, on a bright Tuesday morning, Tony really socked it to 'em – and how! Through the fog of the present, he gave us a vision of a future steeped in sunshine, raining with creativity, thundering with interaction and quite literally drenched in hugely exciting environmental purpose. As the Dome's Spiritual and Youth Adviser, I feel elated, stimulated, electrified – but above all, massively *challenged*.

14 March 1998

Peter is worried that the overall concept might be pitched too high, so eventually we try to make it more consumer friendly by hitting on 'Time to Make a Difference', a hugely exciting state-of-the-art slogan which not only conveys the concept of *time* and of *make* but also the concept of *difference*, not to mention the twinned concepts of *to* and *a*.

But my over-riding task has been to coordinate The Spirit Level, an oasis of calm and reflection that explores the values that underpin our society and how they are expressed through faith and belief, particularly in relation to modern-day spiritual concepts such as All Saints, Crop Circles, Nintendo, top magician David Copperfield, e-mail, UFOs, Princess Di and top supermodel Kate Moss. The kind of essential questions we'll be hoping to pose in visitors' minds are: Who am I? What am I doing here? Who is he? What's he doing? And who on earth are you? Will this take much longer? Can't we give that one a miss? and How do we get out of here?

15 May 1998

To give the New Dome Experience a real taste of the future, we've asked the incredible Peter Gabriel, whose last great hit 'Sledgehammer' reached number four in the charts just twelve short years ago, to put on a prophetic show, with extraordinary shapes created by bubble machines and brilliant fog effects created by dry ice and electric fan-heaters. Raymond Baxter has already agreed to act as compere, Tom Baker will be making a special appearance in his Tardis, and Gary Numan will be performing 'Are Friends Electric?' which was already pretty futuristic in 1979 but will seem even more so now.

45

So an end to carping, all ye cynics. As Tony said, Britain has a long tradition of running down all its ground-breaking projects before they set sail. I mean, once upon a time the snipers even said the *Titanic* could never succeed – and now it's probably the most famous ship in all history. Farewell cynicism! Hail Dome! Hail *Titanic*!

F is for fearlessness

the penis comes of age

Marco Pierre White has one. Martyn Lewis has one. Quentin Tarantino has one. And so does Gavin Strang.

Yes, it's the era of the penis. Not only did Jodie Foster become pregnant without one, but *The Full Monty* received yet a further raft of awards from the Tinseltown money machine without ever even showing one. Meanwhile, the Rt. Hon. John Prescott took his with him all the way to Hull and back . . .

This veritable avalanche of media coverage of the male organ amounts to nothing more nor less than an admission that it is becoming *the* symbol for the way the wind of *zeitgeist* is blowing. Suddenly, the penis is all over the place. Chris Woodhead has one. Richard Branson has one. President Fidel Castro has one. Peter Mandelson has one [COPY-EDITOR PLEASE CHECK]. All in all, penises have come of age.

It's all a far cry from the days when they were buried under the carpet. Nowadays you simply can't avoid them. The *New River Café Cookbook* contains a recipe for Endive, Chicory and Penis Salad with Balsamic Vinegar. The much undervalued Lord Irvine's controversial new William Morris wallpaper includes a recurrent penis *motif* on a purple-and-gold background. The Millennium Dome is set to include a Penis Zone, in which upwards of twelve thousand people an hour will be fitted out in helmets as virtual-reality spermatozoa shoot their way through a larger-than-life replica of a human penis. Teen magazines for young adolescents now regularly feature Fit-the-Penis-to-the-Pop-Star competitions and no one blinks an eyelid. Last Thursday's *Kilroy* programme included studio interviews with eight prominent captains of industry who were prepared to openly admit being worried about the size of their penises. Yes, the penis has finally made its mark.

It all makes my days on the Women's Studies Encounter Unit at Leeds University in the early '60s seem like light years away. For the first eighteen months, we barely mentioned the P-word, though occasionally one of us might imagine what one looked like, and another would sketch her idea of one: I remember making mine a sort of tree, a bit like a sycamore, with birds nesting in it. That's how ignorant we were. Only when the young Jack Straw joined our Women's Studies Encounter Unit on secondment from the Campaign for Real Ale did we really get a chance to find out. My friend Liz was admitted for Trauma Counselling shortly afterwards.

The '70s saw a downgrading of the importance of the penis for penetrative sex. Stroking was in, the penis was out. *The Hite Report* encouraged us to seek alternative uses for penises: novelty kitchen magnets, disposable bicycle pumps, duck-callers. My friend Sue even added some Day-Glo pink material and had one turned into a miniature troll for her mantelpiece collection: sadly, one day she left it too close to the radiator and ever since then it's been a My Little Pony.

Despite the media coverage, these days fewer and fewer women are choosing to use the penis, either for leisure or procreation. Since Christmas, virtually all my kitchen nozzles have been lent out to girlfriends who want to access a baby without male interference. And male genitalia have been eradicated from modern dinner party conversation. Yet in the sixties the penis was a kind of yardstick. No dinner party was complete without someone saying something like, 'The war in Vietnam really freaks me out – it's been going on even longer than my partner's penis.' But in the 1990s it's a conversational no-no.

Yet now, away from selected media, there seems to be what my friend Lyn has called 'a conspiracy of silence around the penis'. Even though statistics suggest anything up to 50% of the world population owns one, the penis is rarely mentioned in Parliament, and you're more likely to read an anagram of it (pines, snipe, spine), even in the *Guardian*, than the word itself. And men are implicated in this conspiracy. When I told my current partner, Don, what I was going to be writing about in this essay, he literally begged me not to put in print just how small and insignificant his was. So I won't, bless him.

Yet I still maintain an affection for the penis. The time has surely come for it to be celebrated rather than eradicated. Jodie Foster might not need one for her pregnancy; Robin Cook might refuse to exhibit his at an impromptu airport photo-opportunity; but please, please, please let's Give Penis a Chance. 'Nuff said.

F is also for Fury

the ongoing debate

I've been a much-loved broadcaster for nearly quarter of a century now – for my sins! – and I've been bringing my wide-ranging experience of current affairs to bear on my current Media Studies course at the University of Oxbridge (formerly Thameside Polytechnic), 'The Three Most Important Words in British Broadcasting: For or Against?'

Unlike some people I could name in this business (now is neither the time nor the place to go into why I ceased working on the consumer programme *That's Life* after an all-too-brief stint as Esther Rantzen's co-presenter in the late 1970s – let's just say that the professionalism was all one-sided) I have always known that conflict must be at the very heart of any successful current affairs programme. My record as a BBC producer speaks volumes. Figures went up sharply when I took over the ailing *Call My Bluff* in the early 1980s, dropped the two old-guard team leaders, replaced them with Germaine Greer and Brian Hayes, and updated its title to the more contemporary and provocative *Stuff Your Bluff*.

On the strength of this, I was promoted to producer of the ailing bygones programme *Going for a Song*. My first act was to jettison the ageing front-man Arthur Negus, replace him with the more vibrant and happening Keith Allen plus team captains Jimmy Nail and (for the older viewer) Janet Street-Porter, and reposition it in the global marketplace as *Shut Your Mouth*, an offbeat panel game in which the winner gets to smash as many valuable keepsakes as he can in the space of twenty seconds.

It was then just a short step to becoming a senior producer of BBC Radio 4's *Today* programme, where every morning opposing teams would hammer out issues of national and international importance in the time allotted. Being a woman, I was made to start on the more anodyne features (typical!). My very first slot was billed as an affectionate look at the Chelsea Flower Show. Luckily, I managed to discover a man in nearby Dulwich who was prepared to come into the studio to argue that he didn't like flowers, that he could see no reason why they should be given so much time, money and media attention, and that, far from being pretty, he felt they were complete and utter eyesores, with an unpleasant odour to boot. With Lady Olga Maitland speaking for the pro-flowers lobby in the radio car ('I'm going to have to rush you there, Lady Olga!'), this made for a very lively and stimulating debate.

My success at fuelling debate meant that before long I was given the 'Thought for the Day' slot to mastermind. The Bishop of Woolwich had already been pencilled in, so there was nothing I could do about that, but I managed to make his thoughts on the need for a little Christian love in our daily lives far more relevant to the radio audience by forcing presenter John Humphrys to interject with hard-hitting, provocative questions like, 'Says who?' and 'So bloody what?'

It was then widely agreed that the weather forecast on Radio 5 Live was badly in need of a massive shake-up, and that I was judged the right person to tackle it. I am now widely credited with having revolutionised the slot, introducing two weather forecasters with opposing predictions about the next day's weather. If one says stormy, the other says sunny spells and if one says windy, the other predicts a

51

calm front. The result? A lively and at times heated weather forecast, fuelling further debate.

Recently, I've landed my own show, and I've been able to inject a lot of this punchy, in-your-face buzz into my Talk Radio phone-in *Give Us a Bel* (5 a.m.–6.30 a.m., alternate Thursdays, check listings for details) by boiling it down to the nitty-gritty. Dangerous driving – for or against? The ozone layer – for or against? Nuclear holocaust – for or against? Child abuse – for or against? These issues have got to be aired – and Talk Radio, 5–6.30 a.m., alternate Thursdays, is the right place to air them.

We aim at a good cross-section of extreme opinion. I usually set the ball rolling with a provocative monologue, designed to tease hard-hitting opinions out of our avid listeners. The other day, it went like this: 'Clinton – for or against? Is Monica a psychopathic liar who should be placed in a straitjacket – or is Clinton a sex-maniac who preys on innocent women? We want to hear your views. The Queen Mother – for or against? Is she a pampered old has-been who should learn to stand on her own two feet – or is she a modern-day saint, who's devoted her life to the service of the poor and needy? Call us now! Gaynor Regan – for or against? Is she a secretary in a million – or is she just a hatchet-faced home-wrecker? I'm Bel Littlejohn – and I want to hear what *you* have to say.' Steamy conflict and heated debate – I'm proud of having steered British Broadcasting towards these two great rocks. But what about you? For or against?

G is for Global Vision

surfing the internet

Are you wired yet? You're not? Hey – get a life, baby! Me, I've been on the Internet for eighteen months now (bel:newlab @nuffsed.zzzz..uk/). Believe me, I've never looked back.

It was my best mate Anita Roddick who first told me to get wired. The Body Shop (smelz:pat.ro.nise.eeeyurgh:uk) has been wired for five years now, so that subscribers can get a generous sample of Anita's lovely new Cocoa and Semolina Elbow-Rub shooting at them down the line – and all for the cost of a local phone call. And let me tell you this, Anita's dream is to link every single Amazonian rainforest dweller to the net, so that they can let her know the minute they run out of Mango and Oatmeal Lobe-Salve and she can barter with them (at a knockdown rate) for extra supplies of Guaca-mole and Red Squirrel Foot Polish.

Let's face it, we're in the middle of an information revo-lution at least as big as Siouxsie and the Banshees – and I'm talking about when they were really big – and yet our so-called leaders appear not to know the first thing about it. For instance, most of my colleagues in New Labour – particu-larly some of the older ones, I regret to say – continue to live in the dark ages. The other day at Walworth Road I was intro-duced to Barbara Castle on a whistle-stop visit. Everyone was telling her how distinguished she was – but then it turned out she didn't have the foggiest idea what on earth a compatible interactive telecommunications interface spread-sheet database was!

'We're talking global visions of an interrelationshipped society here, Barbara,' I told her, but she looked completely blank.

'I trust the present leader of the Party isn't going to abandon good old-fashioned socialist principles – that's all I care about,' she hissed.

'You've lost me there, Barbara,' I replied. 'Say it again, a bit slower this time, if you would.'

As she repeated her sentence, I tapped in *good-sound: soci.priples.uk* into my palmtop. Back came the message, *Refer petman.uk:machi.avel*, and I found myself redirected to my good friend Peter Mandelson's online database.

'Are.we.abandoning.good.sound.socialist.principles?' I tapped into the machine. Sadly, the screen went blank and switched itself off. But as I explained to Barbara, you can't expect a comprehensive international database to carry every single lost detail from hundreds of years ago.

The thing I love about the Net is the way it offers you access to a world of information at the flick of a switch. For instance, if I want to know the bass player of Fleetwood Mac, circa 1969, or the Welsh village with the longest name, or how fast a gazelle can run, or the average annual rainfall in Lima, Peru, or how to cook a vegetarian lasagne, then I can look it up on the Internet. This is incredibly handy for those who can spare the time, even if a book would be quicker.

I can confidently predict that the Internet will change the very nature of Western democracy. After all, who wants to go out and vote in a dusty booth when they can be just as happy staying at home playing on a great little machine? And frankly, I've had some of the most fascinating conversations of my life via e-mail. By linking my fibre-optic interface with an infrastructure of interactive spreadsheet windows, I once even managed to achieve what every buff is aiming for – I was able to talk to myself.

'hi.bel.here.what's.your.@name'

'my.name.wwww.is.bel.too'

'so's.my.name.@.that's.funny'

'maybe.it's.becos: we.are.the.same.person'

'nuff.said.cheers/belUK:over.and.out'

Great! And for God's sake don't tell me you could have conducted a conversation like that ten, fifteen, twenty years ago. It's up to each of us to play our part in taking the information revolution to every home in the country. And let's not be party political about it. Paddy Ashdown's been in the forefront of information technology for a decade now. We in New Labour could learn a thing or two from the guy. For instance, Paddy tells me he regularly updates himself on the latest headcount of Lib Dem MPs by feeding all the available information into his palmtop headcount package and getting an up-to-the-minute read-out. 'It's always around the twenty mark,' he enthuses. He also has valuable information – his wife's christian name and hobbies, his very latest opinions on education – available on a package at the press of a button if ever he needs it. And as for those of us in New Labour, our principal manifesto pledge – 'Guaranteed school places for all nine-year-olds, resources permitting' – remains at the cutting-edge of information technology.

G is also for Grooving

a whiter shade of pale

Hey guys! Let's rock'n'roll!

For me, the history of rock'n'roll begins and ends with Radio Caroline. I was out there from Day One, as studio assistant to Jack Straw, who at that time hosted the popular 'Jack-It-In' show at 2 a.m. every morning, before handing over ('Hi, Dave, how's tricks?') to Dave Lee Travis ('Trix? Now, that's one helluva groovy lady who sounds just my kind of chick – only kiddin', mate – the Hairy Cornflake's doin' just fab!') after the 4.30 a.m. news slot.

Not for nothing was Radio Caroline called Pirate Radio. It was always deeply questioning of society, the cradle for the kind of radical thought that has entered the mainstream of Labour policies under the present leadership. It's by now well known that the young John Prescott was Chief Steward on board Radio Caroline, holding court as that magnificent ship bobbed its way amidst the treacherous storms of the raging North Sea. And it's an open secret that John didn't set much store by the birth of rock'n'roll. 'Blimey O'Reilly!' he would exclaim whenever a fresh photograph of The Beatles was produced. 'Are those birds or blokes?'

This would irritate Jack Straw. Jack liked to wear his hair long, so that it came just over his collar, and with sideburns too. At that time, of course, Jack was in what I called his 'Jason King' phase, all mauves, medallions and frills, though his main medallion bore the head of Keir Hardie, in keeping with Jack's socialist principles.

Ah! The memories come flooding back like ninepins. Petty Officer Prescott – as he then was – spent much of his time trying to 'come down like a ton of bricks' (his own words) on those who flouted the ship's rules, particularly where dirty fingernails, long hair, loud music and illicit substances were concerned. Often he would burst into a studio while the 'ON AIR' light was still on, forcing the disc jockeys in question – Tony Blackburn, Rockin' Maggie Beckett, Emperor Rosko – into an all-over body search while they attempted to carry on broadcasting in a convivial manner. A careful listen to tapes from those live broadcasts of thirty years ago ('And it's a super – ooof – swinging Radio Caroline day – ouch – on your non-stop – leggo – number one music station.') suggests that John inspired a great deal of creative friction from the artistes in question.

Basically, Petty Officer Prescott was a fish out of water, bringing olde-worlde notions of discipline to the casual new world of rock'n'roll. He always expressed a preference for the smooth 'n' easy sounds of James Last and his Orchestra ('at least you can tell he's a fella'), pouncing on anyone he suspected of subversive activity. I'll never forget the day he found Simon Dee and Margaret Beckett lying on a purple bean-bag in their tie-dyes leafing through the *Collected Sayings of Kahlil Gibran* whilst sniffing on a joss-stick.

'To think I went on the Jarrow March for the likes of you,' he said.

'You never,' replied Margaret.

John blushed.

'I were speaking *metaphorically*,' he retorted.

Radio Caroline reached out to the soul of a generation and kissed it better. Without Procul Harum's 'A Whiter Shade of Pale' charting at number 3, it is impossible to imagine the Vietnam War would have ended. Suddenly, our generation realised that change – real change – comes not through speeches or direct action but through popular song. 'Morning Has Broken,' sang Cat Stevens, and a generation laid down its arms and learnt to love.

It's a lesson Old Labour, with all its talk of unions this and wage demands that, somehow failed to master. But Tony and Harriet and Margaret and Jack know better. Radio Caroline taught them to be at ease with themselves. These days, before every meeting of the Cabinet, Tony insists members strip down to their vests and boxers and 'work-out' with Harriet Harman ('Move it to the right!') to music by Crosby, Stills, Nash, Meacher and Young. Clothes back on, we then gather round the table to recite and meditate upon 'Desiderata', or 'New Desiderata' as it has become known since Peter applied his own particular brand of magic to it.

'Go placidly amidst the noise and haste – and remember that the answer to life's confusion lies in drawing up a major discussion document,' we say, as Tony plays the opening bars of 'Classical Gas' on his dummy-guitar. Then it's herbal tea all round. But every now and then, out of the corner of my eye, I see Petty Officer Prescott looking fidgety. 'I could *murder* a cuppa soup,' he muttered last session. Sometimes, it's as if Radio Caroline went down in vain.

H is for Happening

keeping abreast

Now. Just one little word. But it means a helluva lot.

As an arts-lover, I've always been a very Now sort of person. Where reading is concerned, keeping up with what's happening is what it's all about.

Have you read Don Delillo's *Underworld* yet? You really should. It's a literally magnificent evocation of the world in which we live, or in which we would live, if we lived in America. Intensely powerful, hauntingly memorable – and marvellously *dense*. And have you read the new Nick Hornby? So how do you think it compares to the new Don Delillo?

And what about Ted's *Birthday Letters*? I speed-read those poems on the day they first came out, ready to review them on Radio 4's *Kaleidoscope*. Intensely memorable, marvellously haunting, densely powerful. As I said on air, they literally pinned me down to the floor and punched me in the stomach without ever releasing their grip. Later that day I went to a dinner-party where, as you'd expect, everyone else had rushed out and bought the *Birthday Letters*, but I was the only person there who'd managed to get to the end of it in the allotted time. I'm not saying that there are winners and losers in the book-reading world – obviously not – but it

59

was certainly accepted that I had become the natural group-leader in the ensuing discussion.

Needless to say, as the River Café Anchovy Prune Tartlet was passed round, they all looked to me for guidance. 'You mean you haven't read the poem where the plate smashes into a hundred shards, seeming – to me at least – to symbolise the essentially fragile nature of their relationship?' I said. And they had to admit that they hadn't. 'You *haven't?*' I said, arching my eyebrows in sympathy. This was the most Now book of the week – and they still hadn't read one of its most urgent poems!

I want to read Now books – the latest books, the just-out-hot-off-the-presses books, the happening books, the books that are all about what it means to be alive, right here, right Now.

And – you've got it – I want to read them not next week, not the week after, and certainly not the week after that. Yes, I want to read them Now. Of course, some people I could name want to bury their heads in the sand. They see books as an escape from the present, from the Now. Like, three weeks ago I was talking to a colleague and I asked her what book she was reading.

'Jane Austen,' she replied.

'What – the latest Claire Tomalin?' I said. 'Any good?'

'No. Not the biography,' she replied, '*Mansfield Park.*'

'The tie-in book about the making of the latest Merchant/Ivory? Any good?'

'I'm reading *Mansfield Park*, the novel by Jane Austen,' she explained.

'Oh,' I said. Close friends tell me I'm very sensitive to other people's moods: I detected a sad, not-facing-up-to-things expression in her eyes. Perhaps her permanent partner had left her; whatever, she was obviously burying herself in the past, locking herself away in the cocooned fantasy land a million miles from the state of Britain as we fast approach the Millennium.

Like a lot of my close women friends, I am a pivotal

member of a leading reading group in central London. Once a month, we gather around a table with a bottle from Odd-bins to discuss a current book. We try to discuss something everyone else in London is discussing, so that when it comes to discussing it with other people we'll already have discussed it once, and we'll have something to add to the general discussion. Have you read the new William Boyd? How does it compare with the new Fay Weldon? Did you like the bit where – ? Or did you think it was a bit too – ? These are the sort of issues arising out of contemporary novels you must expect to discuss when you meet new colleagues and old contacts, so it's best to prepare for it in your reading group.

As the co-presenter of Radio 4's new daily arts programme *Keeping Abreast*, it's my job to keep listeners up-to-date with all the very latest events and happenings in the world of books. If, say, a new Jeanette Winterson is hot off the presses, then we aim to have it fully processed – read, reviewed, analysed, assessed for its place in the Zeitgeist, discussed, marked on a sliding scale of 1 to 20 and returned to the shelves – all within the space of 24 hours. And let no one claim we don't try to keep in touch with old books: on the Friday of every week, we have a special five-minute slot called 'Classic Fiction' in which we delve into our archives and take the longer view of English literature as a whole, right back to the very beginning of the week, selecting the week's books we think stand a good chance of still being remembered in, say, the year 2000.

As a regular monitor for TV and radio, I'm often asked to name my favourite five books of all time. It's a difficult one, particularly as the list changes every week, with the arrival of newer and more contemporary books, each offering a more up-to-date look at what's really happening in this crazy, fractured, dazzling, sensitive, ugly, beautiful, happy, sad world in which we live. There's no point in recommending the last Martin Amis, for instance, if there's a new one due out in a month's time.

Not long ago, a regular contributor to *The Late Review*, professional in every other respect, said live on air that Philip Roth's *Sabbath's Theater* was one of his favourite books of all time – realising just too late that a newer Roth was expected in a fortnight! He's never been invited back. I last saw him hunched over a half-pint glass of blackcurrant-and-lager in a disused wine bar in Muswell Hill. He had a haunted, out-of-date look on his face. He was reading an Ian McEwan.It was at least six years old.

He hadn't kept up, poor love, and now he's left it too late: no matter how hard he runs, he'll never be able to catch up.

I looked the other way, and hurried past. I thought it kindest.

H is also for Headstrong

a lovely, lovely lady

There's one thing we can all agree on. She's a lovely lady. A truly lovely, lovely lady. One of the loveliest ladies in modern politics. With her Brummie wit and rough-and-ready Brummie charm, Clare Short doesn't have an enemy in the House, except for those who can't stand her. But she's got to learn that being lovely isn't everything when it comes to winning elections. To put it kindly, I sometimes wish she'd take more notice of that timely catchphrase, first coined by the late, great Nye Bevan: 'Why don't you just shut your big fat gob?'

But as I was saying, Clare Short's a lovely lady. I've known her for nearly two decades now, or almost twenty years in metric. She first rose to fame way back in the early 1970s as Clare Long, the Brummie with the heart of gold who co-managed the hairdressing salon at Crossroads motel with Vera Downend in the long-running TV series of the same name. Vera was the toughie, the hard-headed business-woman struggling to drag the salon kicking and screaming into the 1970s with a series of cost-cutting packages and customer drives. And Clare was the more reckless and impulsive one, given to shooting her mouth off at customers then regretting it later.

It led to that special sort of friction which is the stuff of TV drama. In one memorable episode, first broadcast on 11 November 1974, the proprietor of the entire Crossroads complex, Meg Richardson, played by the late Noele Gordon, drops into the salon for a quick perm, as she is expecting a titled guest, Lord Lanchester (who later turns out to be none other than the confidence trickster Sid Bellows). Anyway, Vera Downend is making a tremendous fuss of her boss, making sure the rollers are to her satisfaction and so forth, when the headstrong Clare once again puts her foot in it. 'Blimey,' she pipes up, 'with a face like yours, I don't know why you bother.'

In another episode – first broadcast six months later, in May 1975 – the sauve co-proprietor of the motel, David Hunter, has popped in for a wash and blow-dry. Meanwhile, the then Home Secretary, Roy Jenkins, on a whistle-stop tour of Birmingham, has called in at the salon on a fact-finding tour of small businesses. Greatly impressed by what he sees in the salon, the Home Secretary agrees to a quick trim. But Vera Downend already has her hands full with David Hunter, so she deputes the lovely, headstrong Clare to see to the Home Secretary.

The Home Secretary seems to be accepting Clare's rough Brummie banter ('Blimey, Roy – you're fat and no mistake!') with equanimity. But then the time comes to present him with the bill. In a hurriedly whispered conversation, Vera tells Clare that the Home Secretary's trim is 'on the house'. But Clare isn't having any of it. She wants to charge him double. 'Any road up, 'e can afford it, can't 'e?' she exclaims in her lovely rich Brummie accent.

At this point, the Home Secretary, who has overheard their negotiations, steps into the debate. 'I'm sure we can awwive at some weasonable compwomise,' he purrs. Vera then reminds them both of the principles of collective responsibility. Clare, she maintains, has spoken out of turn. Clare stands corrected, the Home Secretary leaves without paying a penny, Vera re-establishes her authority and David

Hunter, as the co-proprietor with a conscience, insists on paying a full sixty per cent of his total bill.

At this, Clare exits in a huff, just as Benny – played by the struggling young actor John Prescott – enters wearing his familiar woolly hat. 'Blimey – what's up with 'er?' he asks. Vera explains the position. 'Well in my opinion,' concludes Benny with a shake of his head, 'you come to a collective agreement about something, you have a responsibility to observe it. If not, Clare'd better reconsider her future in this salon.' The camera freezes on the shocked face of Vera. Theme music. Titles. End of episode.

Stirring stuff, prophetic in its way, and it's remained in my mind ever since. Who'd've thought that, twenty-one years later, the very same couple – John and Clare – both of them having left Crossroads Motel so many moons ago and both now occupying senior positions at the heart of New Labour, should once again come to blows in such similar circumstances?

As Peter Mandelson has already made plain, New Labour ain't about anything if it ain't about lowering taxes for the better-off, and it's high time Clare – lovely, headstrong Clare – began to realise this. If ever we're going to be able to do anything to help the poor, the homeless, the elderly, the sick and the underprivileged, it'll only be after we've done something to assist the average healthy young family with two cripplingly expensive homes, whopping financial outgoings and the additional burden of two or more children in private education. It's high time Clare learnt the first lesson of life in a motel. Yup, Clare, love – it's finally time to get real.

H is also for Heartbreak

she touched us like a butterfly

It's been a busy week at the University of Oxbridge (formerly Thameside Polytechnic), where I run the Serious Comment section of the Media Studies Course. But it's all grist to my mill: as I say in the brochure, it's my ambition to turn out the next generation of award-winning newspaper commentators like myself, able to express opinions on wide-ranging matters of general importance to the community as a whole.

We had a quiet start to term, with not much happening in the outside world besides the Party Conferences, a couple of natural disasters, a few bombings, some foreign uprisings, a civil war, the Northern Ireland talks and a famine or two. Precious little for the serious commentator to get her teeth into there. So for the first few weeks, I taught an important retrospective course on 'Towards a New Republicanism: Diana – the Semiotics of Grief in the Zeitgeist of a Post-Industrial Society'.

In teaching our students how to respond to this tragic event, I was also teaching them to open up the floodgates of their very own wellsprings of private emotion. To help them, we analysed brilliant texts composed for that tragic week's newspapers by such justly acclaimed authors as Blake

Morrison ('The Princess of All Our Hearts'), Suzanne Moore ('St Diana: a Feminist Socialist for Our Times'), Clive James ('Princess Diana James: it Was Never Meant to Be') and my own justly acclaimed *Guardian* article 'She Reached Out and Touched Us Like a Butterfly'.

But all good things come to an end, and writing about the everlasting and eternal grief we as a nation felt at the untimely and tragic death of Diana had begun to seem like last week's news. After a while, the tears began to dry, the scars began to heal and I could hardly stop myself from screaming, 'So Di's dead and buried – what's new?' At this point, I tried to impress upon my students the fact that grief is a terrible thing, particularly when it's last week's news.

So with the whole Di thing as dead as a dodo, where was the columnist to turn her or his understanding eye? Some of my students started to get desperate and came up with essays on the world economy, or the future of the planet, forcing me to point out that these subjects lack what we in the serious media call colour.

And then – phew! as Himself would say – along came another week with newer news, and at last two real stories for serious comment and consideration. First off, and raising important questions about modern feminism, Britain's role in the world, and culture in the 21st century, was the first leg of the Spice Girls World Tour, jointly sponsored by Pepsi Cola and The Scott Trust. Within hours, my students were studying a variety of think-pieces on the Spice Girls from a cross-section of broadsheet commentators.

In *The Times*, Lord Rees-Mogg had nailed his colours to the mast, stating that, 'Whilst admiring the long-term attractions of Ginger Spice, and being by no means indifferent to the greater genealogical claims of Victoria, I am forced, albeit with some reluctance, to pledge my true allegiance to Scary Spice. I have the very greatest respect for her gifts as a vocalist in the popular manner – her singing voice compares favourably with Pope John XXIII and

President Nixon, both of whom, incidentally, I can write about with personal knowledge – but also for her prowess as a dancer, her skills in this arena calling to mind the movements of Harold Macmillan in his heyday, or even – dare I say it – the footwork of Karl Popper.'

The very next day, Sir Isaiah Berlin, reporting from the concert-hall in Turkey for the *Evening Standard*, took issue with Rees-Mogg. 'For all her undoubted physicality,' he wrote, 'Scary Spice has little of the emotional range of Baby Spice, or even Sporty Spice. In their powerful rendition of "2 Become 1", it is Baby Spice upon whom one's attention inevitably falls.' But this position was immediately condemned in a scathing attack on Baby Spice by Sir Ernst Gombrich in a specially commissioned piece for the *Daily Telegraph*. 'I would have no hesitation,' he stated, 'in declaring Ginger by far the most significant of all the Spice Girls. Her natural vivacity is simply not in question.'

Already reeling from the extent of their Spice Girls in Turkey workload, my students faced further heavy media studies of the battle – recalling the early days of Vietnam – between Chris Evans and Zoe Ball. The main leader in the *Guardian* came down solidly in favour of Chris Evans, a view echoed on other pages by both Hugo Young and Dame Mary Warnock. But the *Financial Times* reported in a special supplement that the markets had responded favourably to the attractive bubbly personality of Zoe Ball, and in the *Independent* Lord Scarman stated that he preferred Zoe's cosier, warmer style. The debate will go on for weeks, if not months, to come, and all serious broadsheet newspapers will continue to give it the in-depth coverage it deserves, together with the necessary pie-charts. One longs to know which side of the divide the lovely Arundhati Roy is on, but for that we will have to wait, with baited breath, for a special supplement to the *Wall Street Times*.

H is also for Horror

you and yours and yours and yours

I've got one helluva lot of time for Jim Boyle, the dynamic and far-sighted new boss of the new-look Radio 4. He's dusted off a lot of cobwebs, blown away a lot of loose baggage and ironed a huge number of shirts – and he's come up with a brilliant new schedule that's not only radical but reforming as well.

His changes are far-reaching and all-embracing. *Desert Island Discs* is to be increased by ten minutes. *Today* is to run for an extra half-hour. Instead of the daily arts programme *Kaleidoscope*, there's a brand new programme, *Scope*, which promises to take a fresh daily look at the arts. We're talking brave, we're talking bold, we're talking shake-up. And that's not all. *Start the Week* and *Midweek* have been given a thorough repackaging by reducing the number of guests from five to four and – in a typically bold twist – keeping on their original presenters.

But boldest and most far-reaching of all is the new, thoroughly revamped consumer rights prog *You and Yours*, to be presented by someone with a proven track record of years of experience in the field, namely myself. It will now run to an hour every day, a far-reaching change reflected in its new-look title, *You and Yours and Yours and Yours*. We aim to include the very best from all the other consumer and minority programmes of recent years, among them ' ', for the deaf, *All Steamed Up*, for those suffering from faulty kettles, saucepans or other general kitchenware problems, *Must Go Now!*, the five-minute slot for people who suffer from compulsive phone-in disorder, and *At Issue*, the lively magazine programme for sufferers from the common cold.

We unveiled the first in the new series of *You and Yours and Yours and Yours* in a special presentation in the Serpentine Gallery yesterday. Why the Serpentine? Because it is situated in London's Hyde Park, the subject of a major special investigation in the months ahead. As I explained to the assembled media yesterday, we were first alerted to the perils lying in wait for the unwary Hyde Park consumer by a postbag of letters from ordinary listeners such as Mrs I. B. Clegg from Knebworth, Herts.

Mrs Clegg explained that she has an occasional allergy to grass. 'The last time I visited Hyde Park,' she continued, 'I was shocked and horrified by the amount of grass that the authorities let grow there, without any apparent concern for the safety of those of us who suffer from similar allergies. I saw no warning signs at all, and no skilled medical staff on hand to deal with the consequences of the authorities' stubborn indifference to the plight of a sorely tried section of the community.'

On closer investigation, we were to discover that an undisclosed number of other citizens had their own horror stories about this park. Mr D. Ranken of Bootle telephoned our Emergency Complaint Hotline to inform us that in the process of conducting his own personal researches, he had come across a very large stretch of lake-style water in Hyde Park. 'There were no signs to tell the public – including many underage kiddies – that this water was unsuitable for drinking,' he pointed out, 'nor had the relevant authorities made any provision whatsoever for those pedestrians who might wish to walk across this sizeable stretch of water. I can only imagine the distress this unprovoked lake might cause an elderly lady with a faulty hip as she attempted to take a short cut across the park, only to find herself knee-deep in damp water. The Government must bring in immediate legislation to resolve this urgent matter for once and for all.'

Ms P. Roberts from Solihull was similarly concerned about the 'quite appalling' amount of large trees she had observed standing entirely stationary in Hyde Park, many of them with potentially lethal foliage. 'A leaf is a potential killer. As few as six-to-seven soggy leaves blown by the wind through the open mouth and into the throat of an otherwise able-bodied human being can choke him or her to death, with heavy funeral expenses, not to mention legal bills for the grieving family.'

In response to these deeply upsetting letters, we on the new-look *You and Yours and Yours and Yours* today launch a hard-hitting Park Alert campaign to draw the attention of ordinary citizens to your statutory rights if and when you suffer untold damage from public parks up and down the country. For this and all the other grim warnings you may require, I urge you – stay tuned.

I is for Indignation

charming? hardly!

His supporters might argue that Hugh Grant is 'just an actor'. Oh, yeah? In fact, Mr Grant and his sidekick Hurley are two of the most blameworthy persons of our times. With their snooty upper-class accents and oh-so-English ways, the sooner they are chucked overboard the better it will be for this beleaguered nation of ours.

It doesn't take an economist to realise that ever since the release of the risible *Four Weddings and a Funeral*, Britain has been going through a severe crisis of identity. Are we part of Europe or are we a separate nation-state? What are we to do about the increasing age of the population as the Millennium approaches? Whatever happened to the promised classless society? Will Rupert Murdoch continue to be allowed to run roughshod over any form of limit to media-ownership? And what about the homeless? And what of Charter 88? Not until the advent of Hugh Grant in his most 'successful' (note the inverted commas) movie did these grave problems hit us where it hurt. But his performance crystallised – and in many ways exacerbated – the British disease of ignoring crises. In fact, you could argue that without the influence of Hugh Grant and his notably Grant-like performances in ruinously popular films, Britain would be a proud, confident young country, topping the economic league of Europe, perhaps the world, with adequate provision for the poor, the disenfranchised, the homeless and the elderly.

As an actor, Hugh Grant is able to take on only two kinds of role: those in which he acts himself, and those in which he doesn't. His films hardly vary either: the ones that aren't set in the present are set in the past, and those that aren't set in America are set in Britain or somewhere else. His own character, too, seems relentlessly the same, as though he were so limited in his imagination that he can only ever conceive of himself as one and the same person. Charming? Hardly. For me, charm amounts to a lot more than a diffident smile, 'perfect' manners, a whimsical haircut and an oh-so-English 'pleasant' demeanour. If you told me Jack Straw MP was charming, I'd agree with you. Or the smashing Margaret Beckett. But Hugh Grant? Nah.

Historians point out that the cracks have been appearing in Hugh Grant's 'perfect' image ever since he was born. His biography is a catalogue of fatal mistakes amounting to an avalanche of indiscretion. He was born into a family that was neither working class nor upper class but somewhere in between. He never recovered. Aged five, he came only third in his primary school egg-and-spoon race. The humiliation would always haunt him. He never recovered. Aged eighteen, he passed three 'A' levels, but Grant knew full well that had he taken two further 'A' levels in subjects he knew nothing about, he could well have faced catastrophic failure. And – on this all commentators are agreed – from this humiliation he would never have recovered.

Disaster followed hard upon disaster, humiliation upon humiliation. As Hugh Grant reached the age of fourteen, he was already a magnet for disaffection and disillusionment. Around him, the Western world was enveloped in a major oil crisis, Watergate was looming and the British nation was forced to struggle through a three-day working week. Yet Grant remained blithely unconcerned. For the young Hugh, it was almost as if he wasn't to blame. By the time Grant was eighteen, the Western economies had plunged into a downward spiral. And Grant's reaction? That same whimsical haircut, that same disingenuously smiley smile.

And what of Elizabeth 'Liz' Hurley? She seems to believe that her tarnished notion of 'glamour' will see her through everything. Ruthlessly seizing every opportunity, she thinks she can just sit back and wait for the world to owe her a living. But we're not all like you, Liz. If ever I go to a new movie – the latest Ken Loach for preference – I might just don something patchworky and a little bit ethnic I bought three years ago half-price in the Monsoon sale. But I'd never parade my body around the local Odeon half-naked in Versace. And nor would Harriet Harman. Has La Hurley never heard of the word self-effacement? Bel Littlejohn thinks not.

I too have been a successful actor in my time (as Cath in the 1975 semi-professional rehearsed reading of Wesker's *The Kitchen* at the Theatre Upstairs, Market Harborough) and as a senior political thinker I've been subjected to the full glare of the media spotlight for over fifteen years. So let me give this tip to Grant and Hurley: sorry, but we're not interested in you any more, we're not remotely obsessed by your sexy outfits, your glossy smiles and your boring career moves. And these days, let's face it, who would even bother to write about you? Yup: sorry, loves, but it's over, *it's over*.

I is also for Involvement

words are our syringes

If I see a stooped figure outside my nearest superstore (have you tried the new freeze-dried Waitrose Vegetarian Tikka Masala with Sultanas and Lemongrass? It's to die for) rattling a collecting box for this charity or that, I never pass them by without giving them a huge great big smile of encouragement, a smile that says, 'I'm with you all the way, but sadly I've got my last-minute shopping to do – must rush!'

And from the way they look back at me – serious, concerned, their faces wreathed in sorrow but now with a renewed sense of optimism – I think they admire me for *making the effort*. For them, as for me. Good Karma is half the battle won.

And, in all modesty, I can see how their spotting Ms Bel Littlejohn of the *Guardian* makes all the difference in the world, keeping them going through the sleet and the snow, knowing that they can return home soaking wet and tell their partner 'Guess who smiled on me today – Bel Littlejohn from the *Guardian* – a very busy and concerned lady, but never too busy for a smile', or words to that effect.

And it's about charity that I address myself now. Or rather

one 'charity' in particular (note the ironic quotation marks – and remember also that I am recognised as the supreme mistress of irony!). Yup, you've got it – Mother Teresa and her Sisters of Charity. Anyone who read the searing *Guardian* piece about her so-called organisation, or who has read Chris Hitchens' remarkably measured biography of that lady, *Worse Than Hitler*, will know quite how dreadful it is. As the article said, there's one feature about Mother Teresa that really sticks in the gullet: she's only interested in keeping them alive.

Fact: Her homes have far too many people in them, and a lot of them are really not well enough for ordinary decent helpers to mix with. That article spelt out the fact in damning detail that one of her homes alone has greedily allowed in 50,000 people since it opened in 1952 – small wonder room service is so slack.

Fact: There are no CDs in her homes, no woks, no Extra Virgin Oil, no French films on video, precious few modern novels, no duvets, no sun-ray lamps, no focaccia bread. I suppose the lady thinks, in her Almighty way, that these basic commodities are *just that little bit too good* for her lowly clientele.

Fact: Mother Teresa *ignores all Western medical advice* and, in her high-handed arrogant way, *can't bloody well be bothered to put factor 15 sun-lotion on her face* – hence the leathery skin and mass of wrinkles.

Fact: Far from being the self-proclaimed 'little old lady who has devoted her life to the good of others', Mother Teresa is a PR supremo brilliantly skilled at manipulating the media. After Hitchens' book appeared, she cold-bloodedly refused to appear on *Start The Week*, the *Late Show*, *Wogan* and *Noel's House Party*, thus deftly turning his attack on her to her advantage. Makes you think, eh?

And while this diminutive PR wizard is gallivanting around on an ego trip, dragging the less-well-off into her homes and then denying them access to all kinds of visual and intellectual stimulation (the new Bertolucci is *still* not available in Calcutta, despite repeated requests from many influential people in the London media), we leading columnists at the *Guardian* are doing our level best to make this ailing world get well soon. Opinions are our first-aid kits, paragraphs our pills, words our syringes, photo-bylines our bandages; and we do whatever we can, come rain or shine, to make our opinions available to whoever should be in need of them. Unlike Mother Teresa, who, when she's not forcing the sick to lie down in her homes, just swaggers around the chat-show circuit looking 'holy'.

But then, I'm a people person, and that's a term that would mean nothing to Mother You-Know-Who. 'Nuff said.

J is for Jolly Interesting

a day in my life, and then another

There's so much to read in the papers, there really is. That's not to say there isn't room for improvement. Personally, I wish there were more foreign news in the broadsheets, but then that's just the kind of person I am – serious, thoughtful and with my own far-reaching perspective on world affairs. Frankly, I would have become a foreign correspondent if I hadn't thought I could do a helluva lot more good as an award-winning columnist.

And while we're on the subject, I'm sorry, but I'm sick to death of stories about the royal family. If I have to read another article on Charles and Camilla or Andrew and Fergie I think I'll scream. I mean, why should we be interested in what Camilla has for breakfast, or what colour Fergie is choosing to paint her new whirlpool bath?

(Actually, the answer to the first is 'Just a large cup of herbal tea and perhaps a Ryvita', and to the second 'pale blue with a hint of peach' – but frankly, who cares? But what I'd like to know is this – is one Ryvita enough, particularly with her busy schedule? And how can Fergie afford a new whirlpool bath anyway? It's high time we were given answers to these questions.) Incidentally, I learnt the other day from someone who really knows that Prince Edward is trying to cut down on sugar in his coffee and has taken up the sugar-substitute Canderel – a fact I've yet to see reported in any paper: so much for good reporting!

My best part of any newspaper, if I'm being really honest, is not the foreign news or politics or health or even environmental catastrophes. No: my absolute fave part is the women columnists, especially those who aren't ashamed to tell us exactly what's been happening in their private lives, warts and all. Needless to say, I've had plenty of requests from lovely, lovely readers asking me to do the same. 'Bell,' they say, 'you're a fount of wisdom and terrific source of informed comment on national and international news – but please, please, *please*, Bel, tell us a bit more about *yourself.*' So here goes: A Day in the Life of Britain's Most Concerned Columnist.

Yesterday, I woke up at 7.21 a.m., and after booting His Nibs out of our shared bed, I made my way to the kitchen. We have knocked two rooms into one, thus making a combined kitchen/dining area, which definitely makes much more sense in the long run. I made myself a cup of tea, but when I poured the milk it floated in globs to the surface. I realised at once that it was off. On the radio, they were talking about the Northern Ireland situation, and whether in the long run the two nations would be united, which might make more sense. I switched over to Radio 2. I then took a teaspoon and tried to fish the globs from the top of the tea, but with only partial success. I then decided to have a cup of coffee instead; I don't mind coffee without milk but I hate tea without milk. I put one-and-a-half spoons of Gold Blend into the blue mug with the chip on it and then I put a sugar-substitute in it and waited a minute for it to cool.

A few minutes later, I began to sip my coffee. It tasted quite coffee-ish. On the radio, they were discussing the single currency, so I switched back to Radio 4. I was halfway through my coffee when I decided to make a piece of toast. I did this by cutting a slice of bread off a fresh loaf with a sharp knife and then placing it in the toaster.

I have found over the years that this is a good method, as it means both sides can be toasted at once, and at equal heat. The toast completed, I spread it with Olivio, an effective butter substitute to which I am devoted, and a thin layer of thick-cut orange marmalade made to an excellent recipe by the late, great Elizabeth David, given to me recently by a close friend, Barbara, when she came to stay. On the radio, news came through of either a famine or a drought in either Africa or India, I didn't catch which. My marmalade on toast was delicious, but my left hand was a bit sticky. So I turned on the cold tap and gave it a good clean. On the radio, they were discussing the future of Russia under an ailing Yeltsin. This set me to wondering whether it wouldn't be better for my health to drink herbal tea every morning.

And isn't it about time I invested in a whirlpool bath? They say they're completely fab, though obviously one would have to go for the right colour. The announcer said that news had just come in of a major pile-up involving ten cars, so I switched back to Radio 2, wondering whether the day would be hot enough to wear my beloved old Katherine Hamnett Nuclear Awareness T-shirt . . .

Still just 7.35 a.m., and six hundred words later I've hardly even finished breakfast! As I have long suspected, the details of my day-to-day life are proving a very rich source of inspiration for this award-winning column. Soon I'll tell you what it's like getting dressed, and later you'll learn all about the way I brush my teeth, and after that . . . but I mustn't ruin it for you.

K is for Keeping in Touch

info-mation

The news? It's a vital part of all our lives. 'I read the news today, oh boy,' sang the late, great John Lennon. Even we ordinary mortals use the word 'news' all the time in our day-to-day conversation, as in 'What's on *the news*, Jack?' Hang on, Deirdre, I must just catch *the news*' and 'Any *news*, Tony, of the recent record-breaking pile-up on the M1?'

I usually start my news day with a regular fix of the *Today* programme. I really never feel fully alive and 'raring to go' until I've tuned into their up-to-the-minute news of the latest natural disasters, disputes, wars, famines, crises and motorway pile-ups. While I'm working and when I'm in the car, I tune to Radio 5 Live, always on the alert to catch anything truly awful that's happened between the main news bulletins. If, say, a Briton has been injured in a train accident, or, say, twenty-five Americans have been massacred by a lone gunman, or upwards of five hundred Indians have died in a flood, then I may well make a note of it, as it could well be something on which I'll be expected to comment in one of the leading news programmes, or even in my newspaper column.

News, news, news: I don't mind admitting it's seen me

through many a personal crisis. For instance, when things were going badly for me as Assistant Editor (Sadness, Traumas and Upsets) on *Cosmopolitan* magazine back in the early 1970s, I took great solace from keeping in touch with all the atrocities happening in Uganda, particularly to Britons. It made me see my own problems in perspective, and I would set off each morning with a new spring in my step, ready to face the problems of the day ahead. Vietnam, Watergate, The Falklands, Desert Storm, and – truly unforgettable – the Tragic Death of Diana, Princess of Wales: these are events of worldwide significance that have kept me glued to my radio and/or television, on the hour, every hour, simply grasping for all the latest in the way of news, views, live footage, comment and just-breaking, solid gold infotainment.

And so to the King of News. I've known John Birt ever since we worked together on the consistently under-rated *Bruce's Big News Night* (LWT) in the mid-1970s. As you'll remember, it was a brave attempt to bring more and more news to more and more viewers by having it presented by Bruce Forsyth. We chose Forsyth for the job because we knew no other all-round family entertainer who could present the world news with such authority. One week, Bruce would be reporting live from Peking on the death of Chairman Mao (or 'Chairman Miaow, naughty puss' as Bruce would insist on calling him!) and the next he would be cross-questioning the two rivals for the American Presidency with the special help of Rod Hull and Emu and The Roly-Polys.

This was just one of John's many brave attempts to extend the boundaries of broadcast news. And now comes his boldest plan yet with the launch of News 24, the 24-hour non-stop channel of rolling news. It's widely known in broadcasting circles that John has asked me in as a special adviser to News 24, bringing to it my unquenchable enthusiasm for all news, the tragic, the near-tragic and the not-quite-so-tragic.

From what I've seen so far, News 24 is set to fulfil a truly vital role, offering viewers up-to-the-minute coverage of all the stories that are breaking, some that have already broken, and others that you have to work at with a hammer and chisel before they break. I've made some major improvements. The presenters were already in the middle of the newsroom, rather than in some poxy, stand-offish little 'studio', but to heighten the feeling of immediacy I got them to take off their jackets and roll up their sleeves. I've further insisted that the heating in the newsroom is turned up twenty degrees. This gives the viewer a real impression of hot news, delivered fresh out of the oven of international conflict.

And it's working. Take one particular 24-hour period, for instance. On a disappointing day – no major tragedies to Britons, only a handful to Americans and Europeans – our News 24 dry-run focused on the breaking story of ex-Chancellor Kenneth Clarke taking a holiday from Euro-intrigue to enjoy a quiet day at home. What was the ex-Chancellor thinking? Over to our Economics Editor. As Clarke sat at home, was he nursing a grievance? Over to our Political Editor. Was he likely to stroll down to his 'local' at lunchtime for a quiet pint? Over to our fly-on-the-wall team at The Cricketers. What are the medical dangers, if any, of drinking at lunchtime? Over to our Medical Correspondent. Might the ex-Chancellor then take a walk in the countryside with a trusted political ally? Our Environment Editor was ready with the roving camera crew in a neighbouring field, sending back the latest info-mation, as it became available, on the ex-Chancellor's most likely route.

As it happened, word came through at 17.02 hours that the ex-Chancellor wasn't at home in fact, but had spent the day in the City. At last we had a major story, contradicting all our previous predictions: proof positive that News 24 is set to bring you all the news as it happens – and as it doesn't happen.

L is for Love of Animals

hands off monsieur reynard

Me? I'm an animal-lover, and frankly I don't give a damn who knows it. From the largest whale to the smallest hen – I love them all. Hens – and baby chicks with their lovely soft feathers and their cute, cuddle-me expressions – are a particular passion of mine. Let me assure you this much: if ever a little bitty cluck cluck clucky henny-wen wenny is hurt, you will find Bel Littlejohn sobbing at her side.

I was arguing my great love of the animal kingdom over the Sunday roast chicken with couscous and River Café Shredded Parsnip with Ginger last weekend. The topic of conversation? You got it. Tony and New Labour's brave decision finally and at last to pursue a total and utter ban on all forms of the vicious so-called 'sport' of foxhunting.

Yesterday saw a few hundred of the remaining (secretly funded) dinosaurs of the pro-hunting lobby gathering in Hyde Park for a pathetic yet blood-curdling rally. Inevitably, the assembled speakers – mainly toffee-nosed, chinless-wonder Old Etonians in expensive tweeds, their estates funded by their bastard ancestors' ill-gotten gains in the slave trade – tried to make out that those of us in the anti-blood-sport camp are motivated by class hatred.

What nonsense! Frankly, I don't give a damn how these

upper-class twits, Lloyds' losers, serial adulterers, snooty layabouts and self-confessed wife-beaters choose to get their rocks off. They're a dying breed, and how they choose to die is no concern of mine. But what I *do* care about is the well-being of the fox. Even the thought of a single fox in pain makes me want to cry my heart out, and then some.

I first fell in love with Monsieur Reynard when I was a little girl of eight or nine years of age. I had been given that marvellous children's book *Ferdinand the Fox Goes to the Farm* by Father Christmas. Within the space of just two paragraphs, I was positively swooning. And by the final page, the young Bel was deeply in love.

As you may remember, the book revolves around a visit made by the dashing Ferdinand the Fox to his local farm. Avoiding the shepherd, he manages to climb his way over a stile, and then slither under a fence until he is in a field with thirty lovely little baby lambs. How Ferdinand smiles to see these lovely little baby lambs at their antics! He laughs good naturedly as they gambol to and fro between their mummies – and permits himself a sympathetic chuckle when their little legs seem to fall from under them and they roll down the hillocks in lovely cuddly bundles!

Ferdinand the Fox then bids farewell to his furry friends the lambs, and hastens to his chums the hens with a spring in his step. 'Hello, Ferdie!' clucks Henrietta Hen delightedly. 'Come and meet all my little chicks!'

Ferdinand's eyes fill with tears of joy as he spies the eight-nine-ten little chicks that his dear old friend Henrietta has given birth to. 'Why, Henrietta!' he exclaims with a foxy wink. 'Surely, they are the cheekiest little chickety-chick-chicks I've ever seen!'

The story ends on a sad note – Ferdinand bites the throats off all the chicks and leaves Henrietta without a head before going back and finishing off the lambs – but I ignore all that. The book was written in the olden days, the days before authors could be expected to grasp the need for tact, care and relevance in children's literature. The one thing that has remained with me down the years is my love of not just the furry, forceful yet fanciful and funny Ferdinand, but all fabulous furry foxes everywhere. And I will fight tooth and nail to see that their right to roam is preserved from the braying cruelty of the toffee-nosed brigade.

Ordinary working-class folk – many of them very dear friends of mine – don't care much for hunting. Why should they? It's got nothing to do with class. It's just that they're not cruel, silver-spoon-in-mouth, castle-dwelling, Lord Lucan-style psychopaths.

They prefer an ordinary, decent sport like fishing. There's nothing they like more than to sit with their feet up by the side of a river or stream while at the other end of their line a fiesty fish flips and flops, splishes and splashes, and strives to assert his carefree *joie de vivre* to his heart's content.

Unlike in cruel fox-hunting, it is well known that the fish themselves love this honest, working-class sport. Not only does it give Freddy Fish a bit of healthy exercise – plus all the fun and challenge of extricating himself from that mischievous line! – but it also affords the poor old water-bound creature a unique opportunity to get out of the water for a while and take a lovely long look around at the fields and the meadows before being humanely coshed and placed in a wickerwork basket, woven, more likely than not, by a local craftsman.

So well done, Tony. If all goes well, in a month or two the huntsmen will have been taken down a peg or two, those wicked, wicked hounds will be enjoying a lie-down on the vet's couch, and all those dear ickle lambs and chick-chick-chickies will be looking forward to a visit from plucky old Uncle Reynard. Bless him.

M is for Mild-Mannered

blowing their noses for them

That was a brave decision, and I am truly glad to be associated with the newspaper that made it. And nice timing, too. I'm talking, of course, about the *Guardian*'s courageous stand in giving Mr Gerry Adams space to put over his point of view to tie in with the IRA explosion in Canary Wharf. Shame, in a way, that they couldn't have printed it a day or two earlier, so as to get people in the right mood for the explosion. Sometimes, if you explain these things beforehand, then ordinary decent people – newsagents, shop assistants or whatever, people not yet wholly 'politicised' – feel much more at ease when they actually happen.

One thing Gerry made absolutely clear in that tough, straight-talking article was that he absolutely disapproves of violence in any shape or form, and would only ever sanction the murder of innocent men and women if he felt it wholly necessary to the successful advancement of a non-violent society based on cooperation and democracy. Frankly, I wept buckets – *buckets* – when I read Gerry revealing how his thoughts were first and foremost with the victims, because that's the kind of guy Gerry is, always thinking about his victims, old and new, past, present and future.

Take it from me, I know Belfast and its people. So often

people talk about the 'Northern Ireland Situation' who don't, but I do. I was in that tormented yet magical island for a long wine-tasting weekend in 1971, and I was going to go again for a Van Morrison concert just six years ago – you don't give up on a whole people just because of the threat of a few explosions, you know – but in the end I had to cancel at the last minute owing to a suspected security scare, and I bought a live album instead.

Unlike other so-called 'experts' I am steeped in the history and politics of the Northern Ireland situation: it was all in a memorable poem by Seamus Heaney a few years ago, I forget its exact title, but I read it all the way through. Believe me, this sort of intimate knowledge and – yes – abiding love of a country and its literature never really leaves you. And so when I am asked, as a senior commentator, broadcaster and opinion-former, to comment on the delicate Northern Ireland situation, I attack the question with a depth of informed passion ('In the words of the Paul McCartney song, let's for God's Sake give Ulster back to the Northern Irish!' I announced bravely on *Question Time* last week) that gives some of my fellow panellists – a lot of them just locals, unaware of the larger international issues involved – a much-needed kick.

Back to Gerry. Believe me, he's a genuinely lovely guy who hates to see a little child blown to pieces in a necessary if regrettable retaliatory gesture against the stubborn post-colonial aspirations of a discredited British government. His moving article in Monday's newspaper offers generous comfort to the parents and friends of his victims. 'At this time my thoughts are with the families of those killed and injured,' he writes, movingly, 'I understand the pain they are going through.' Personally, I hope someone out there will embroider these beautiful words on a lovely Northern Irish linen tea-cloth, so that those of us who are forced to live away from that war-torn province can hang them over our Agas and look to them for succour in our darkest hours.

Can I share some very personal tales about Gerry? As a

schoolboy, he proved himself a great leader of men. When his fellow pupils would start to kick one of the more obstreperous new boys in the shins, Gerry would remain clam and thoughtful. 'It is wholly regrettable to me that this action was provoked by the unwarranted attitudes of the young lad in question, who must bear total responsibility for the collapse of the non-shin-kicking agreement,' he would announce, viewing the kickings with an understanding smile, enjoying them, yes, but never condoning them. 'Nevertheless,' he went on, 'we remain firmly committed to a democratic means of resolving issues and to the objective of an equitable agreement that will command the consent of all.'

As a young man, he always had a tremendous sense of occasion, insisting on nipping down to the barber to have his hair re-layered before waving his men off to do battle against the forces of imperialism. Yet he was also endearingly self-effacing, taking pains that others less well known than himself should be seen at the head of a Troops Out march, particularly if it seemed possible the glory of full-scale battle involving death and injury might be theirs to treasure.

From an early age, Gerry has been tremendously cultured. He likes to go home after a busy day orchestrating retaliatory gestures against the occupying forces to his fireside and his collection of quietly moving Chekhov short stories. It was no doubt the inner humanity gained from his love of literature that inspired him to write that great, heart-stopping line in the *Guardian*: 'It is crucial that people sit down around the table and treat each other as human beings.' And, believe me, no one knows better than Gerry what a human being looks like, alive or – well – not so alive. We're behind you, Gerry!

M is also for Mind-Blowing

my all-time top 500 cds ever in the history of the world

My personal Top 500 best ever albums of all time in the history of the world bar none? That's the question I'm always being asked by friends, fellow experts and devoted readers, bless 'em. Of course, it's an impossible choice, leading to much head-banging. For instance, I've had to leave out Seizure's seminal *Kick My Head In Til It Hurtz*, even though it would undoubtedly make my list of Top 10 best ever albums of all time from West Hartlepool. And it's caused me many a sleepless night and countless tears having to exclude Acne's remarkable *Acne IV* album (1979) in favour of Roy Harper's neglected 1971 classic *Songs I Discovered Deep In My Beard*. Meanwhile, how can I exclude Iggy Pop's raw, urgent masterpiece *Urine in My Slacks* (1980), even if it lacks the raw urgency of his earlier *Shooting Up Weetabix* (1973)?

But my Top 500 is now stacked in strict alphabetical order in my album and CD library. Of course, like most of the other rock experts who've been devoting the past six months to compiling the official *Guardian* Music of the Millennium, my alphabetical order is not based on the name of the album or band, but exclusively on the christian name of the all-important bass-player. This system is complicated by my chance discovery that forty-three per cent of all rock

90

bass-players are called 'Bob'. This means 212 of my Top 500 albums are listed under 'B', and another 56 under 'C' for Chris. But when you know as much about rock music as I do, you know the huge debt we all owe to the guy in jeans and a T-shirt in the background slogging out his guts on the four-string.

Over the past month, I've been cross-indexing my Top 500 for easy reference. And I've come up with some fascinating facts which add interest to my forthcoming *History of British Rock Volume 12*, 1969–71 (Macmillan, £25, 770pp). For instance, on the third track of the second side of the first disc of the magisterial triple-album *Embarking on an Astral Voyage with the Children of Eden* by Yes, the single note on the mouth-organ you can just hear at the end of the line 'And now we flee, my masters and me, to a land of dreamy oblongs' is in fact played by Frank Gurn jr – who was of course also the percussionist on the second solo album by Scraggy 'The Hulk' Smith after he broke with Deep Purple citing musical differences following their famously ill-fated tour of Italy in 1968, on which, incidentally, the legendary blues guitarist Murky Hollow memorably duetted on the Turin gig with the then unknown Pete Tosh, who was acting as backing vocalist for supporting band Blood Transfusion, whose *Blood Transfusion VII* album is now widely believed to have featured Leon Russell on keyboards, under the pseudonym of 'Boz Chink' – the real name, as you know, of the bassist with Soiled Fish on their *Live at the Marquee* album (1977) who was later to die in an aircrash exactly three years, one month and two and a half weeks to the day after Jimi Hendrix also met his untimely death. And it's my enthusiasm for unearthing amazing coincidences like this that keeps me on the cutting-edge of rock criticism.

Unlike many of my contemporaries, I have not, thank God, surrendered to the downhill-all-the-way-since-the-Beatles mentality. When I started out in journalism on *NME* in 1969, my fellow rock and pop journalists included Peter Sissons (Heavy Metal), Polly Toynbee (Country and

Western) and Donald Dewar (Blues). Among our rivals, the Alan Beith Interview was the weekly highlight of *Sounds* magazine, and Alan was the first British journalist to interview Janis Joplin. But since then, they've all sold out, turning their back on their rock roots, putting on their suits and ties, settling into secure Establishment lives, with their Volvos in the drive and their Dire Straits' CDs on the mantelpiece. Sad, really.

But I still go crazy for rock. And, yes, I still get tremendously excited by extraordinary new bands of the calibre of Pulp, Bed Sores, Stomach Pump, Burp, Stink and The Prodigy. If ever I feel that life is getting a drag, I schlepp up to the CD player and place something truly mind-blowing like *Never Mind the Bollocks* by the Sex Pistols or *Fuck Off You Prick* by Buttock full blast on the turntable. Then I go into the next room, shut the door, put the cushions over my ears and make myself a lovely warm milky drink. And I'm careful to keep my finger on the pulse of true innovation: I'm always eager to hear from my secretary Rowena, bless her, what it's like to listen to some of the greatest new sounds around, including new albums by Radiohead, Garbage, Warty Tongue and Puke.

And it's to preserve this incredible sense of youthful thrill that next year the Directors of The Scott Trust are set to expand our brief current list of 100 to your all-time best ever 10,000 top albums. By the end, we'll have a playlist comprising upwards of your 100,000 all-time best ever top tracks. And did you know that Fairport Convention's Dave Swarbrick can be heard saying, 'When do we start, man?' on the second track, side two, of The Strawbs third album? Tell that to the young today, and they'll never believe you.

M is also for Misery

xmas à la bel

Merry? Hardly. Scientifically conducted studies by literally millions of leading doctors and academics have conclusively proved that far from being festive, the Yuletide season is in fact one of the most miserable times of the year. And it's not just the rampant consumerism: tempers fray, friends and family fall out, the well of human happiness runs dry, there's wrapping paper all over the place and no amount of scrubbing can remove the gravy stain from your new Katharine Hammett dungarees

We're going for a minimalist Yule this year. To add a dash of Brit-art to the proceedings, I've splashed out on the new Gillian Wearing Xmas video, showing once again her mother and daughter arguing and sobbing, only this time in party hats. Towards the end, a Father Christmas figure comes in and chokes them both to death, which is symbolic. Luckily, Gillian made the video on a loop, so that it can play in the background all through Xmas day, without having to reach for the restart button.

And we've cut back on the Xmas tree, too. For years, we've selfishly robbed the Earth of one of her fir-covered children, but this year we've taken the eco-option and made our own tree from lots of bits of timber. And what of the spiritual side? Sadly, Yuletide has been taken over and exploited by the religious lobby, but I have no desire to use it as a vehicle for my beliefs. Broadly speaking – and let's not go into detail – I believe that there is a – how should I describe it? – well, a *thing* out there, bigger than us all, but still manageable, some sort of present or presence, a kind of *unseen force* which is a lot more powerful than we are, but which doesn't speak much, if at all. But I really don't see why I should ram this hard-won belief down everyone else's throat. For that reason, I maintain a strictly non-sectarian Xmas household.

We won't be having a female angel on top of our tree, this year, for instance, even though a reviewer of my recent book *The Ongoing Process: a Biography of Jack Straw* was good enough to say that I wrote like an angel, or words to that effect ('She writes at an angle' *New Statesman*). Female angels have sexist overtones, and Camille Paglia is among those who have realised that making them sit on the pointy bit at the top of a tree for the Yuletide period is an act of misogyny. Instead, I have felt-tipped a pair of thick-rimmed spectacles on an Action Man and dressed him up in a lightweight grey suit, so that we now have our own Home Secretary looking down on us from a great height throughout the Yuletide season, making sure that we are all in bed at the appointed hour and not taking any harmful drugs or subverting the ordinary, decent, fair-minded norms that Tony has blessed us with.

Of course, Xmas is a time when we exchange consumer durables and luxury items with each other in return for goods of a similar value. For my daughter, I shall be buying books that reflect life as it is lived in present-day Britain, including *Dismal Days in the Tower Block* by Ted Needham, which won this year's prestigious Paracetamol Prize for Children's Literature. It tells the tale of Danny, who can't think of anything to do in the dismal tower block of the title. After nearly ten minutes of searching, and still finding nothing to do, he decides to go indoors and switch on the telly, as it's only forty-five minutes until *Neighbours* – a happy ending, yes, but a happy ending that arises from the text rather than being imposed on it from above by an authoritarian author.

Another great book for kids – pessimistic yet despairing, bitterly sad yet grimly realistic – is *Stella and the Dragon* by Lyn Smith. It's about a kid of seven, the child of separated parents, who encounters a great big green dragon, spouting fire from its nose, and has only a stick with which to fight it. Stella bravely brandishes her stick, shouts 'Take that, Mr Dragon!', and is sadly eaten by the dragon in two quick bites. I admire this book for the way the author refuses to take the easy solution of letting the kid escape through some absurd magic trick, instead forcing the young reader to confront death in an adult world.

Cooking throughout Yuletide is always a problem, and I hope that my new seasonal cookbook *Coping with Xmas* (Hodder, £7.95) takes some of the strain away, turning a potential nightmare into a simple chore. My best tip for Xmas lunch? Forget the turkey, do away with the so-called Xmas pudding (historically a comparatively recent invention – and an unwelcome throwback to the British Empire), and serve sandwiches instead. Then in the evening you can recycle the unused sandwiches by putting them under the grill, perhaps with an inexpensive cheese topping.

As a member of the steering committee of the New Millennium Dome Experience, I am strongly pushing Peter M to reserve one section for 'Future Xmas'. It will, I think, be beautifully stark and minimalist, with all the current Yuletide vulgarity – the decorations, the so-called presents, the ersatz snow, the commercialised pantos, the Santas with all their horrible yo-ho-hoing – swept right away. And in their place? Adult discussion groups interacting with one another, tackling serious issues in an adult, listening sort of way. It's a dream, yes – but a dream worth the struggle. Until then, I wish you an Endurable Xmas, and a workable New Year.

M is also for Moisturiser

kiwi fruit ear-foam

Knock it off, guys. It's twenty-two years since the lovely, lovely Anita Roddick opened her very first Body Shop, and good luck to her. But instead of celebrating her great achievement in making Peppermint and Wine Gum Ankle Lotion available to the ordinary man and woman in the street, her self-styled critics are slagging her off.

But let's take a trip back in time to 1976, when, like you, I was ten years younger than I am today. What would you have found in my bathroom in that long, hot summer of '76? A bottle of Silvikrin, a bar of Camay, a tube of Macleans and not much else. But these days, I've had to put in a couple of extra shelves for my Body Shop products, including Jojoba and Smoked Salmon Lip Gel, Spinach Toothpaste, Lettuce Leaf Neck Scrub, Nettle and Artichoke Shower Foam, Camomile Tea Bottom Cleanser, Rum and Raisin Moisturising Spirit, Porridge Oats, Poached Egg and Fried Slice Face Mask, Kiwi Fruit Ear-Foam, Beetroot and Bran Flakes Hairspray, Honeyed Beeswax and Calves' Liver Navel Rub, Ham Salad Knee Scrub, Pressed Goldfish Facial Mask, Keir Hardie Yucca Hair Conditioner, Asparagus and Sauce Hollandaise Eau de Toilette, Fruit Gum Face Balm, Mule Perspiration Lobe Massage Cream, Marmoset Nostril

97

Gloss, Chicken Tikka Masala All-Over Cleansing Milk, Lark and Juniper Neck Sorbet and Che Guevara Depilatory Lotion with Vitamin E.

'Nuff said. Anita has changed the whole way we live and breathe. It's hard to imagine we could ever have lived without Anita's brilliant Mau-Mau Knee Scrub, but somehow we got by. And not only that, but she has changed the way we think about the environment. For instance, before I saw Anita talking so passionately on our television screens, I would never have thought of becoming a fully-fledged American Express cardholder, but that was what her advertisements did for me, and frankly, I now never leave home without it. Thanks a bundle, Anita – I owe you one.

But there's a lot more to Anita Roddick than mere personal hygiene. Let me tell you this. She's saved over 3,000 blue whales worldwide simply by refusing to go ahead with plans to sell a Blue Whale Foot Lotion, even though her chief executives advised her that by applying it to one's feet and placing them under water one could communicate with friends in baths up to two miles away. In the same way, she refused point-blank to stock a highly marketable all-over Mongo-Mongo shampoo and shower gel made from the ear of the South-East Australian mongoose, and in so doing has ensured the continued sharp hearing of over 30,000 mongeese, for whom hearing aids with their attendant wires and batteries could have proved prohibitively expensive.

Her campaigns are now legendary. In all modesty, I have had a hand in one or two of them myself. I well remember Anita ringing me up one sunny morning just as I was scraping off my Phlegm of Young Aristocrat Walnut Facial Scrub to ask me if I'd write her a notice to display in the front windows of Body Shops worldwide condemning the intransigent attitude of the British Government to the plight of the Jojoba Indians of South America. 'We have so much to learn from these people, Bel, if only we'd give them the time,' she said. I asked her what we could learn. 'I really didn't have the time to ask them,' she explained, 'but I think they may possess the wisdom of the ancient secret of the perfect wash-and-go hand lotion.'

In recent months, Anita has stepped up her campaign against the forward march of the global multinationals and the increasing homogenisation of international merchandising by sticking up identical protest notices in her 1,300 outlets worldwide (1,421 by the end of this year, if her current multi-million-pound expansion runs according to plan).

And this is where yours truly comes in. As is widely known, my public relations company, Bel and Frendz, has been asscciated with The Body Shop for ten years now. In fact, in her fascinating autobiography, *Busy Body* (1992), Anita listed me as one of the six greatest influences on her life, along with Verdi, Rousseau, Harriet Harman, the Dalai Lama and Snoopy. So Anita and I have been banging our heads together to come up with some truly fantastic ideas for celebrating The Body Shop as it enters – can you believe it?! – its third decade.

I don't want to give away all the surprises up our sleeves, but let me just disclose how we've managed to entice one or two very senior New Labour figures on board for a joint promotion. After all, both Anita and Tony share the same broad ideas of a stakeholder society and personal cleanliness. Have you ever seen Tony poorly shaven, or with so much as a blemish on his skin? Likewise, have you ever seen Anita snatching away a stake in society from a Jojoba Indian? 'Nuff said.

Let me tell you one or two of our exciting joint ventures. Gordon Brown has agreed to celebrate Body Day by taking our All-Over Tangerine and Fizzy Lemonade Body Rub to the Despatch Box, while the lovely, lovely Peter Mandelson is all set for a six-month session with a leading member of the Vitamin B Shower Gel Tribe of East Africa. Happy Birthday, Anita – let's boogie!

N is for Nostalgia

the walrus was roy

Na na na na-na-na-na, na-na-na-na, na na. Na na na na-na-na-na, na-na-na-na, na na. Na na na na-na-na-na, na-na-na-na, na na. Na na na – you know, I could go on like this for ever. You don't need to tell me – by now you're singing along with that truly unforgettable chorus from the immortal 'Hey Jude'. Magic!

I have particular cause for celebrating the Fab Four. I was one of those privileged to be a member of the original backing chorus in those Abbey Road jam sessions. Thoughtfully, Paul had felt-tipped a large placard for those who might find difficulty remembering all the words – 'NA NA NA NA-NA-NA-NA, NA-NA-NA-NA, NA NA' – and an additional special audio-cassette for those (Brian Jones, Tony Blackburn, Keith Moon, the young Barbara Follett) who fell into the twin categories of not being able to remember the words and not being able to read them either. The rest of us just sang our hearts out, putting all the meaning we could muster into those deceptively simple lyrics.

You'll remember the film of the event. There was everything our great big beautiful universe could throw up: bubble-machines, dry-ice, joss-sticks, the lot. I was with my then husband Michael Meacher. At that time Mike was a real head-freak heavily into tie-dye. Now, of course he is a leading light in New Labour, always taking care to wear a sober shirt, jacket and tie over his purple haze neckless sloop-shirt. But sometimes when he's up on the Front Bench arguing seasonal export figures with his opposite number I can see his fingers drumming out an old riff like the one on 'Whole Lotta Love', using the Despatch Box as dummy-keyboard. In fact, during a late-evening debate at the end of the last Parliamentary session, I could tell he had an old Rick Wakeman number on his brain. I knew this because halfway through his reply to the Government White Paper he called for another despatch box to be set up at right-angles to his own. He then proceeded to hammer out Rick Wakeman's magical 'Journey to the Centre of the Earth' in its entirety, refusing all questions from the floor lest they interfere with the flow.

But the influence of The Beatles spreads even further. None of us who were there for the recording of 'I am the Walrus' will ever forget all the other heads, dressed in a variety of crazy outfits, singing their hearts out for a world of love and peace. Who was the Walrus? That's been a question on the lips of rock historians these past twenty-five years. But now I can tell you.

The Walrus was Roy.

Roy Hattersley had been invited along to the recording session in his lightweight white polo-neck and cowboy boots on the understanding that he would mime along with the background chorus. Alas, Roy had never been backward in coming forward, and just as each session was really getting going, he would wave his hands to stop the orchestra. He'd then chip in with a variety of questions and objections. 'Erm – excuse me, Mr Lennon,' he would interject, 'but might I ask – and, as one who immersed himself in the Bard from his earliest years, I feel duly qualified in so asking – whether, on the profoundest level, these words reflect the full range of human experience or do they rather, if you will forgive me for opining . . .' Finally, the group had little choice but to pull the Walrus novelty-mask firmly over Roy's face, thus creating the enigma that has lasted ever since.

And the influence on the man remains: those who have played the tape of Roy's speech to this year's New Labour conference backwards have been able to detect that self-same Beatles' chorus popping up between pauses: 'For I believe that a proper education is no less than the very birth-right of any youngster born in this country, *goo goo ga-joo, goo goo ga goo-goo-joo,* and we will not lightly be forgiven if we seek to deny that insurmountable fact.' (*My italics.*)

Those fantastic memories of the Fab Four come flooding back. Like my good friend the lovely Janet Street-Porter, I still keep my finger firmly on the pulse of modern music. Let me assure you it's not dead yet. Great sounds are coming from groups like Blur and Oasis and loads of others such as Blur and Oasis and many more: Oasis and Blur to name but two. But all these great new bands would be the first to admit that they're just pale imitations of The Beatles. And of course, everyone remembers where they were when they heard John Lennon was dead. Me? I was in my car. Or maybe at home. Or conceivably on holiday abroad with one or other of my husbands. Na na na na-na-na-na: truly, memories are made of this.

O is for on the take

a liar and a cheat

Go get him, lads – and then give him a kick in the groin from Bel! That was my first thought on seeing the *Guardian* headline. 'A liar and a cheat' – that's telling it like it is! For far too long we ordinary decent voters have been subjected to the heartless bullying tactics of Tory MPs. Now at last we had one of 'em nailed, good and proper, begging for his life.

But Hamilton's activities – and the tough but very sensitive and breathtakingly cultured *Guardian* editor's noble and to my mind utterly praiseworthy chastisement of their perpetrator – raise the much larger issue of the way people will do anything to suck up to those in power. As the senior *Guardian* columnist with special responsibilities for issues of private conscience and public morality, I first became aware of Tory sleaze rumours in the late 1980s whilst holidaying in the Bahamas, courtesy of British Airways and the excellent Travel-in-Style Suitcase plc. On that smashing winter break (beautifully smooth flight, and my set of Travel-in-Style suitcases is still going strong) I noticed, over the other side of the swimming-pool, a backbench Tory MP and his lady friend sipping what looked suspiciously like champagne on their sun-loungers. The word 'corruption' was swift to raise its ugly head. How could this Tory MP afford this sort of jet-set high-life on a backbencher's salary? This is a question that demands to be answered in an open society.

And it was this very question that I put to my then partner (whose identity, incidentally, is a purely private matter between him, if it was a him, and me, if it was me). My partner (BA's double-tickets are a swift and easy solution to holiday problems – thanx guys!) said that the Tory MP and his wife (if she was his wife – we all know about Tories going on holiday with people they're not exactly married to!!) were obviously 'on the take'. We both agreed that there's no such thing as a free holiday. No one gets a holiday of this calibre without having to sing for their supper.

I had no actual proof that this Tory was in the pay of this or that travel firm – how could I, given the web of secrecy he had constructed? – but I compiled a list of ten questions I wanted the Prime Minister to put to him in an emergency session the moment his plane touched down at Heathrow. 1) Who bought your Ambre Solaire? 2) How much did it cost? 3) What do you mean you don't know how much it cost? 4) Do you really expect me to believe that? 5) And who's that woman with you? 6) So where's the marriage certificate? 7) Did you and your so-called 'wife' write a thank-you letter for your holiday? 8) If not, why not? 9) Are you really no better than a slug – yes or no? 10) If you're not guilty, why am I asking you questions like these?

Back home, putting the finishing touches to my hard-hitting travel piece ('Pack Your Travel-in-Style Bag for the Romantic BA Holiday of a Lifetime' by Bel Littlejohn, *Guardian*, October 19 1989) and grappling for hours with losing this and that on expenses, I got to worrying about the moral and financial turpitude endemic in our political system. MPs of all parties seem prepared to stab any colleague in the back in the fight for promotion.

By this time, I had, of course, risen to the giddy heights of Chief Leader Writer – the previous incumbent had been forced to resign after the editor had been informed by an anonymous source – known only as 'BL' – that he was plotting for his job. My new role placed me in an excellent position to set the world of politics to rights – and about time too! Though I say it my self, my editorials acquired a legendary status among my peers for their moral force and integrity.

My first contribution roundly castigated the Thatcher government for the gross immorality of its plans for a poll tax. 'It is our deepest wish that any local government tax should prove itself as efficient, sturdy and long-lasting as a Travel-in-Style suitcase,' I boomed. 'And if Mr Ridley, Mrs Thatcher and the rest of the motley Tory crew want advice on top-class management, we suggest they apply to the excellent management-training scheme run by the excellent British Airways.'

But the Hamilton case makes me wonder whether my words were not written in vain. And I am not alone. At the delicious dinner for journalists provided at this week's launch of the fabulous new Oxo Tower Restaurant, the talk turned to the way politicians have succumbed to the wicked 'something-for-nothing' philosophy inherent in Thatcherism. The so-called 'cash-for-questions' scandal raises vital questions (which I posed in a freelance article for the *Evening Standard*, and again on LBC) about the sincerity of our MPs. But if there's one thing I can't stand about this sordid affair, it is the Hamilton lobby's supreme self-righteousness. 'Nuff said.

O is also for Outdated Obsession

the whole class thing

Could someone please, please tell me why the British are so obsessed by the whole class thing? There's no room for uppers, lowers and middles under Tony B, thank God. Nor for upper-middles, lower-uppers or upper-lower-middles for that matter. In New Labour, we're heartily sick and tired of the whole outdated concept. Except perhaps for John Prescott, who was middle-lower and then rose through upper-lower and upper-lower-middle to become middle-middle or even upper-middle-middle, and is consequently obsessed by it. And who can blame him, with a background like his?

Just when you thought the British obsession with the whole class nonsense was at long last under wraps, along comes a new TV series called – you guessed it! – Class. I mean, honestly! Isn't it about time we forgot about it? You'll certainly never find a senior radical writer churning out that corny old standard 'Whither Class in the 1990s?' when there are so many more challenges facing us as we approach the New Millennium: how to reduce class sizes by two and yet still remain within budget, the implementation of our 'Quicker to Prison' scheme for persistent young offenders, and so on.

But, just this once, let's ask ourselves the question: in the 1990s, whither class? I'm lucky enough to live and work among people for whom the whole class thing is dead and buried. Consequently, I'm just as happy to have a jolly good barney for a few seconds at the end of every other day with my hard-pressed secretary Rowena as I am to engage one of Her Majesty's Secretaries of State in wide-ranging discussion over lunch at The Ivy. (Obviously I try to avoid politics with Rowena. She's the only person I know who voted Conservative, except for the (black) man with the peaked cap on the door of the *Guardian* building, name forgotten.)

There were representatives of every single class (*must* we use that word?) at a recent party to celebrate the triumph of Emily's List at the Folletts' semi-detached house in a middling-style stretch of Cheyne Walk, just opposite inner-city Battersea. It was well up to the standard of party the Kinnocks used to throw in the '80s, with everyone there you could ever want to meet. I tell you, no one cared a jot about who ranked higher than who – we were all just there to have fun for a New Britain! As I was saying to the formidable John Birt (who incidentally seemed tremendously excited by my off-the-cuff proposal for a new six-parter, *Bel Appetit!: Cooking the Littlejohn Way*), it's high time we did away with this debilitating notion of a social pecking-order, where person A is worth more of your time than person B who is worth more than person C, etcetera. But at that point Melvyn B came over and beckoned John away for a quiet word, so I never got a chance to ram my point home.

Barbara F had kindly invited some of her hard-pressed constituency workers, bless 'em, into her own home for the party. They'd already honed their skills handing around election literature to the ordinary folk of Stevenage, so they were well-placed to circulate with the dim-sum, leaving Barbara's loyal and inexpensive staff to cope with the drinks. One or two of them even mixed for a few minutes with Barbara's high-flying London friends – quite a thrill, and hats off to Barbara for not stepping in!

'I'm excited, Tony's excited, Gordon's excited – everyone in Britain's excited! And the weather's great too!' I was saying to Tessa Blackstone while the lovely Filipino waitress hovered around, waiting for a suitable moment to refill our glasses. 'And the Spice Girls are doing brilliantly in America, and we won the cricket, and–and–and apparently they just *adore* Robin Cook in Madrid.'

There was – *is* – that sort of mood in the air. There's a wholly democratic, classless wind sweeping the country. Yup, we've all got the wind, and it's something I'm hoping to celebrate at Gordon's first major summer drinks party in the garden of Number 11. Obviously, he can't ask all his close friends, so he's restricting it to his most influential mates in journalism and broadcasting, as well as key players in the Cabinet and one or two major figures from the world of film and television. If this doesn't leave room for the Michael Meachers of this world, well, *tough*, frankly.

Of course, he's had to disappoint one or two old chums, it's inevitable. I've heard that Neil and Glenys, for instance, are bitterly disappointed not to have received invites. But you have to draw the line somewhere. For all I know, they may be very good at their little jobs, bless 'em, but sadly a Welsh transport commissioner and his wife are no longer essential to any really important gathering, bless 'em! As Peter M points out, if we passionately want to get this country back on its feet again – and my God we do – then we've got to take some pretty stark decisions, starting with who is and who isn't invited to what. That's the only way we'll truly create a totally caring, totally equal society – a society where at long last the Upper House is filled with centre-left people like us, and outdated nonsense about 'class' doesn't get a look-in.

P is for Passion

new labour's mr darcy

It was while watching the smouldering Clark Gable in *Gone with the Wind* the other night that the thought struck me. The same haughty sneer, the same full, pouting, sensual lips, the same shimmeringly sexual hips, the same take me! take me! look in his eyes. *My God*, I thought, *it's the Chancellor! It's Gordon Brown!*

Gordon Brown is the steamy sex symbol of the Government, oozing political reform. He's the silent, brooding Mr Darcy of New Labour. The term 'shake-up' might have been invented for him. Most women I know – and a few guys! – wouldn't half fancy a shake-up with Gordon.

I had been intending to discuss the implications of the Devolution Referendum on long-term prospects for a Single Currency with particular regard to the recent French elections. But then I thought – to hell with it! Frankly, there's not a single senior political commentator who can concentrate on higher matters while Gordon Brown is leaning suggestively over the Despatch Box, his breath heavy with moody plans to take his gut instincts one stage further. Next week, The Scott Trust, of which I am Deputy Chair, will be unveiling its plans for a major summer *Guardian* promotion. Having collected twelve tokens, answered three questions and completed the statement, 'Gordon Brown is the dreamiest Chancellor ever in the whole world because . . .' in no more than twenty-five words, the lucky winner will be treated to a candlelit dinner for two at the River Café with the Chancellor. He/she will also receive two personally autographed full-colour photographs of Gordon in jogging gear – yours to treasure for always as a memento of a truly fabulous night out.

What exactly *is* it about Gordon Brown? To me, he looks like the kind of boyfriend who would arrange your airline tickets, talk to your accountant, help you decide what books to read and what dress to wear, stand back to let you through doors first and tell you who to vote for. This may sound anti-feminist, but is in fact very, very feminist indeed, 'cos it leaves you with more time to think about truly important things like current films, eating out and looking great. He would be an ideal boyfriend, because you would feel safe in his firm, masculine but wholly sensitive hands, clean but not too clean, with the occasional bit of dirt nestling between his fingernails, and the soft, slightly pudgy, yet still vibrant skin beneath.

This is a man who would never wear gardening gloves to mow the lawn. Nor would he take a bath in his boxer-shorts, always preferring to splash about in the fully glory of his own nakedness. Yet beneath that bullish, manly exterior beats a warm, pining heart. This is a guy who would never ever sit smack on top of a sweet old lady if there was a spare seat on the double-decker.

Here's ten things you never knew about Gorgeous Gordon:

- Though a snappy dresser, he has never worn a flowery tie: he suffers from hay-fever.

- On hot days, he employs Skin Protection Cream Factor 12 – but he continues to draw the line at wearing lipstick.

- His surname – Brown – is one of the most popular in

Britain. His parents and grandparents also went by this name. Some people spell it with a final 'e' – but not unpretentious Gordon.

• It is not true that he does not get on well with Robin Cook. Quite the reverse. They often attend fancy dress parties together in the guise of The Blues Brothers – and are guaranteed to set the party rocking with laughter with their brilliant synchronised dancing to great upbeat tracks such as Wilson Pickett's 'Midnight Hour'.

• He can entertain friends by talking about 'indigenous growth' for a full minute without hesitation, deviation or repetition – whilst simultaneously downing a pint of McEwans from a straight glass.

• He chose saucy French song 'Je T'Aime, Moi Non Plus' for his Desert Island Disc – and threatened to walk out when starchy Radio 4 presenter Sue Lawley refused to dance to it on the studio table.

• He was once engaged to Princess Anne's younger sister Jacqueline – and Palace sources confirm that the Duke of Edinburgh regards him as the strong and forthright son he never had.

• His first action on reaching Number 11 was to cancel his subscription to *Smash Hits* magazine – he was furious at their continued refusal to feature an interview with top Scottish band Runrig.

• He keeps his hair in good condition by washing it regularly with Alberto Balsam Shampoo for Men – and he never goes anywhere without his battery-operated blow-drier for added body.

• His decision to keep his mouth open between sentences stems from a traumatic fly-swallowing incident when aged twelve.

111

P is also for Protest

you gotta serve somebody

Days long gone . . . but, mmmm, the memory lives on. I remember sitting on a purple bean-bag with Jack Straw in the late '60s, me on folk-guitar, Jack on maracas, Robin Cook on organ, Harriet Harmany (as she then was) on kazoo, the four of us singing great old Woody Guthrie protest songs until way into the early evening.

'This land is your land, this land is my land, this land is made for you and me.' Those were the days of hope, days when we really believed we could change things by song: but it was to be nearly thirty years before 1 May 1997, the day those early dreams were to become a glowing reality. 'The answer, my friend,' I remember singing to myself at the end of that momentous week in British politics, 'is one of many options soon to be considered in a provisional draft discussion document.' As a lyric, it needed a certain amount of work done on it – but it truly encapsulated the burning hopes of a generation.

We now have the truly wicked news that Billy Bragg has written the melodies for fifteen previously undiscovered Wood Guthrie songs – tidings of great joy to those of us who were involved in the whole protest thing right from the very start. Do you remember Paris '68, the joy, the liberation, the burning sense of revolution in the air? For those of us in the thick of it – I was just a few hundred miles away at the time, in Eastbourne, working for one of the most radical florists of his generation – it was like a dream come true. And it was the protest songs of that year that kept our radical flames burning. Who could ever forget Dylan's searingly angry rendering of 'Hey, Mr Tambourine Man', in which the singer bumps into a man in the street with a tambourine and demands that he 'play a song for me', adding, 'in that something something morning I'll come da-da-di-da'? Believe me, it's etched on all our minds.

And protest songs remain a very potent influence in our land. They can carry a political message simply and clearly right into the hearts and minds of millions of listeners. It is by now widely acknowledged that it was the sheer force and passion of Billy Bragg's protest songs during the Miners' Strike of 1984 that brought the Tories crashing to such a humiliating defeat in the General Election of 1997. For this reason, the much-maligned Peter Mandelson – who, incidentally, loves to hum radical old Barbra Streisand numbers to himself while he's pedalling away on his new exercise bike – has been commissioning a series of brand-new protest songs for and on behalf of the Government in time for the New Millennium.

Already, some of them have come in. Frankly, they are so truly passionate and cutting-edge that I just couldn't resist sharing them with you today. Last night, thirty years on, the old gang – Robin and Harriet and Jack and Myself – sat around, jackets unbuttoned, in Robin's Foreign Office Snug, belting them out at the tops of our voices.

'Hey! This is a great one!' enthused Jack, dressed in his best casual wear, with tie-dye cravat, earth-shoes and a pair of his favourite loons. 'It's a reworking of a Peter, Paul and Mary favourite with an incredibly up-to-the-minute new message specifically designed to access the young.' He then got out his maracas and sang, sang, sang:

113

'Puff the Magic Dragon
Lived by the sea
Until picked up by armed officers
Working undercover for the CID . . .'

Great song, great rendition – and with a tremendously powerful message for the kids of today, bless 'em. Then it was Robin's turn to blow our minds with this forceful re-working of the classic Woody Guthrie number, written in full collaboration with the lovely Madeleine Albright (ex-Mamas and Papas):

This land is your land?
This land is my land!
This land was made for me, not you.

After a short tribute song to the pioneering Derry Irvine ('We Shall Overcharge'), Harriet knocked us all backwards with a scorching, heartfelt version of Dylan's 'You Gotta Serve Somebody', which we all dedicated to Tony. Finally, I told the gang that when Peter had asked me to compose an anthem for the opening of the Millennium Dome, it had been the proudest moment of my life. He was after something as powerful as D-Ream's election anthem, but with a cutting-edge, futuristic, Millennium twist to it, reflecting the responsibilities of three years in Government. My solution?

Things can only get better!
Can only get better!
Or a little bit worse!

You'll be hearing this chant a lot in the next three years. Enjoy!

P is also for Public Relations

an image transformed

'You know, there's an awful lot of people in pain out there in this huge, frightening world of ours, and it's up to each and every one of us to do something about it.' This was the slogan I chose way back in 1989, when I set up my public relations company, Bel & Frendz. And it's a slogan that's as relevant today as it ever was. Perhaps more so.

Obviously, we at Bel & Frendz PLC continue to do our bit for the poor. As recently as 1992, in conjunction with Anita Roddick, we flew two and half tons of Peach, Juniper and White Chocolate Neck Scrub and Shower Gel to the former Yugoslavia. But we also go out of our way to act for clients who may be experiencing grave hardship in the glare of the world's media. The rich and famous can suffer pain too, you know. Just because you're featured in *Hello!* magazine – for which publication, incidentally, I have a lot of respect – it doesn't mean you're not hurting deep down inside.

This is where good public relations comes in. Bel & Frendz encourages the media to view our clients in a better light. We have transformed the public perception of many of my clients, lending a more positive image to, among others, the Water Companies, Paula Yates, The Al Fayed Group, Vladimir Zhirinovsky, Hillary Clinton, David Montgomery, the Newbury by-pass, Michael Winner and Sizewell C.

And I'm glad to have done the same for my long-term client – and close personal friend – The Duchess of York. It is by now widely known that Sarah contacted me shortly after her tragic separation from The Duke of York with a view to re-establishing her name as a quality product in the highly competitive international Royal marketplace.

As soon as the contract between us had been negotiated, I immediately warmed to Sarah. Together, we set about creating a 10-point plan to offer the general public a more positive view of her character and capabilities. This is the sort of dynamic approach to the media that requires an established reputation in PR.

'I see you as a strong woman, an independent woman, a woman who craves glamour and affection,' I told her, 'so we must get rid of your rather stuffy, frumpy, Duchessy image.' As a means towards this end, we at Bel & Frendz fixed that she should greatly enhance her media persona by appearing topless in the arms of a new boyfriend, preferably an American.

As I assured Sarah at the time ('Wipe away those tears, love'), those original toe-sucking photographs made a huge impact on the world market, upgrading her status from Royal frump to international jet-set celebrity overnight and thus confirming her as a Royal market-leader. We then set about capitalising on this sea-change in public perception by generating a suitable product to assist in large-scale revenue creation. 'I'm thinking a book, I'm thinking a children's book, I'm thinking a children's book we can write in the morning and get drawn in the afternoon,' I said.

'Crikey!' she replied. Then she furrowed her brow and whooped, 'How about "Grungie the Manic Depressive"? No? "Cruddie the Bulimic"? No? "Drudgie the Mother's Help"? No?' She was close to tears, and hurting dreadfully. 'Oh, Bel – you'll have to help me!' And so 'Budgie the Helicopter' was born. It was fully dictated by midday and illustrated by teatime – and the rest is publishing history, or would be if it were more historic.

After Budgie, I gave Sarah a complete fashion makeover. We decided that the Princess Di 'sporty' look was for her, so she would turn up at boxing gyms wearing a T-shirt with a cheery slogan ('DUCHESSES DO IT ON THE PISTE'), lime-green Lycra pants and waders. 'Whatever you do, love, always walk with your mouth wide open,' I advised, ''cos that way you'll be projecting a "mouth-wide-open" image. The public will love it – just look what it did for Donald Duck.'

I taught Sarah how to keep herself in the public eye by spending at least three times her total income. 'That way they'll adore the way you're a girl who's out for fun, fun, fun – and then they'll feel desperately sorry for you when the bubble bursts. The public loves a loser – that's our philosophy at Bel & Frendz,' I explained.

Our overall marketing strategy for the Duchess has already started to pay rich dividends. Sometimes I think PR is as valuable to those who suffer in public as any amount of medicine could ever be. Future plans for the Duchess? My lips are sealed, but if you said, 'Work-Out Video, Fergie Diet Manual and Miss Royal Wet T-Shirt Competition,' you wouldn't be too far wrong. Yup. We have lift-off!

Q is for Questions Only Art Can Answer

i wish i could disappear now and for ever into the ground, buried and forgotten

It asks questions. Big questions. Broad questions. Tall questions. Questions over three-quarters of a mile long and nearly forty metres wide. Yup. I'm talking about the 1997 Turner Prize exhibition.

The talk in the judges' room – interactive, challenging, *inherently disturbing* – revolved around the three key questions facing us today. 'Who are we? What's it all about? Why are we here?' I asked halfway through, my voice pitched on a tightrope between jubilation and abject despair.

The Secretary of State looked at his agenda papers. 'I'm Chris Smith, you must be Bel Littlejohn,' he said, 'and this is the Turner Prize selection committee. We're here to choose a winner.'

The four finalists had in a deeply disturbing way touched on some of the biggest issues inherent in our society. I wanted this to be recognised by the committee.

'At issue –' I said.

'Bless you,' said Chris.

'At issue,' I continued, 'are major questions about identity, life, death, and the nature of art. It strikes me that Gillian Wearing produces work that yields insights, both funny and *disturbing*, into the complexities of life at the end of the 20th century. On the other hand, Christine Borlands' funny and *disturbing* pieces yield complex insights into life at the end of the 20th century, while in her highly innovative work Angela Bulloch raises questions that yield insights into the complexities of life, both funny and *disturbing*, at the end of the 20th century. At the other end of the scale, I think Cornelia Parker's complex insights into life at the end of the 20th century are, in a very real way, both funny and *disturbing*. Frankly, all four artists are so radically different, I really don't know which one to choose.'

Incidentally, it's widely acknowledged that had I not been a judge myself, my own, much-praised Serpentine exhibition 'I Wish I Could Disappear Now and For Ever Into the Ground, Buried and Forgotten', with its controversial, *disturbing* exhibit of mucus from the noses of over three thousand dead garden worms, rearranged on glass and spread into a six-foot-long copy of my own autograph, would have been a strong contender for the Turner.

Like many of those on this year's Turner shortlist, I am literally obsessed with death. My installation piece, 'Cage', shows the skeletons of eighty-three hamsters positioned neatly in a great big hamster-wheel, ten foot by ten foot. To me, it says a lot about death, a lot about human captivity, a lot about our relationship to the environment at the end of the 20th century, a lot about our collective memory (what were the names of these creatures? what did they do in their lives? did they get much exercise? what were their mothers called? – *these were real hamsters once*), and a lot about the process whereby society heightens its recontextualisation of available resources in order to negate the very process it seeks to serve. But above all it says one helluva lot about mortality, and quite a bit about hamsters.

Like Gillian Wearing, my show revealed me at the cutting-edge of video art at the end of the 20th century. I'm probably best known for my video installation 'Seventeen Minutes' Fury: Confusion, Destruction, Geranium'. This is the famous video of an ordinary housewife trapped in a trolley, wheeled around a supermarket by a man with a carrier bag over his head past literally thousands of late-20th century consumer items, replayed over and over again, with a soundtrack in reverse, at once brutally funny and compassionate yet strangely *disturbing*.

I'm glad to say that *Time Out*'s perceptive critic Sarah Kent recognised the final moment of this installation, in which the trolley tips over, releasing the ordinary housewife (or is she an ordinary housewife? what exactly is 'ordinary'? who is a wife? what is a house?) from her trolley/prison with only slight head injuries, as 'one of the great defining moments in post-war art, a howl of ecstatic liberation from the reductionism of consumerism in a recontextualised world that is at once disturbingly permanent yet inherently fragile, a fitting monument, brutal and powerful, to the artist's obsession with mortality. In exposing our fears and fantasies, she strikes raw nerves.'

Sitting in that committee room, we debated long and hard over which of the four artists had produced the most disturbing exhibition. Nick Serota, bless him, confessed that he found Cornelia Parker's work 'very, very disturbing', but I finally won the day for Gillian's work when I confessed to finding it 'very, very, *very* disturbing'.

So it was a good week for contemporary British art. The Turner Prize has put conceptual art right back where it belongs in the headlines of the British press, just three pages along from the Spencer divorce, and only a little way below a new photo of a grieving Paula Yates. And Gillian Wearing goes away from the lavish award-dinner, attended by some of the wealthiest and most prestigious names in the art world, with a £20,000 cheque – which should enable her to come up with yet more disturbing questions about privilege, consumerism and the nature of art in the late 20th century.

R is for Ravenous

the cannibal within us all

Hotel du Vin, Winchester: one of our more intelligent critics once pointed out, in his review of my serious study of the swelling number of American mass-murderers *Packets of Serials* (1993), that – and I quote – 'Every sentence that Bel Littlejohn writes is yet another barrage of gunshot in her long and enduring battle with words.'

High praise, indeed. Yet I repeat it not to blow my own trumpet (let's leave that particular occupation to grown men and other little boys), but to show that when a writer like me turns her attention to murder it is for a very serious purpose. I proved this five years ago with my investigation into the maternal psychological roots of the mass-murders in Milwaukee, *The Dahmer Drama: Mama's Karma* (1990). More and more sensitive, quality writers such as myself are turning our talents to exploring the mind of the murderer, with full-colour illustrations.

These days, murder is not to be sniffed at. Here at Winchester Crown Court, a stunning array of award-winning writers is already lined up for the trial of Rosemary West, ready to write that which cannot be put into words. Next to me sits Brian Masters, who wrote the definitive work on Denis Nilsen, *Pot Noodle* (1984), and who is proud to

121

number many of our leading serial-killers among his pen friends. Other writers who are set to produce serious psycho-anthro-sociological studies of the West trial include Barry Bloom, author of *Leaving Something For Mr Manners*, about the Wisconsin cannibal serial-killer; Fay Scrivener, whose penetrating reports for *New Yorker* magazine on the trial of the one-legged Nevada serial-killer, *Hopping For A Reprieve*, earned her the Pulitzer Prize; and Norman Mailer, whose bestselling study of Gary Gilmore, *The Executioner's Song*, was described by one leading critic as 'sizzling'.

None of my own studies of murderers has been about killing *per se*. Instead, they have been chilling indictments – which are, to my mind, the very best kind of indictments – of the kind of society in which such stories can flourish. Why then are we so fascinated by murder and cannibalism, however highbrow we may be?

In each of us resides a cannibal. In his own book on Dahmer, Brian Masters quotes the renowned French psycho-therapist Alfred Bogusse, who stated that 'Every man and woman experiences, at one time or another, a gluttonous craving for a stranger's kidneys, more often than not gently sautéd with onion and a little bacon. But most of us have been socialised by a repressive culture to sublimate such yearnings. It is only the honest man, the man who has refused to cut the umbilical cord to his own inner needs, who possesses the courage to have a jolly good tuck-in.'

Perhaps my own experience at the Hotel du Vin might shed some light on this controversial claim. Yesterday, we all assembled for the opening day of the trial of Mrs West. In a spirit of authorly camaraderie, Brian suggested we join one another for dinner. I sat between Brian and Norman Mailer, with Fay Scrivener and Professor Barry Bloom on the other side.

It was while we were waiting for the warm salad of goose liver and shallots, with a citrus-fruit butter sauce wrapped in a blackberry and apricot parfait, to appear that I felt an unusual sort of nibbling sensation towards the bottom of my left leg. At first I ignored it, spread some more butter on my bread, and attempted to engage Norman Mailer in a conversation about where, from an aesthetic point of view, one should place the main murder in one's book. Should it be at the beginning, in the middle, or at the end, so the reader has something to look forward to?

Norman was telling me he always likes to place his killings at regular intervals throughout a book, and that henceforth he wouldn't take on a commission unless the serial-killer in question had been sufficiently hard-working to produce what he called 'a nice even spread'. But just then the nibbling began to turn into something more closely resembling a full-blooded chew. 'Excuse me, Norman,' I said. Picking up the tablecloth I looked down to see Brian Masters on his knees, napkin wrapped neatly around his neck, digging his teeth into my upper shin.

'Brian!' I exclaimed, but to no avail. By now, he was busily shaking the salt and pepper over the shin, and spreading it with a slightly fruity tapenade of Mediterranean olives. 'Brian!' I exclaimed louder, and this time he stopped.

'I trust you're not asking me to deny my natural urges, Bel,' he said. 'How awfully *bourgeois* of you.'

It was then that I realised how right he was. As writers, we must empathise with our subjects, come what may, so I let him continue. This means that when I enter the courtroom, I will be on crutches, but with discreet if extensive bandaging. But what is art without suffering? And what is the point of a killing, if a killing can't be made?

S is for Sensitivity

fiction: the way forward

Sensitive? Literary? You bet. Over the years, I've often been described as 'our most acutely sensitive literary critic'. Whilst less sensitive critics can only manage 100–150 pages a day, I can read two, three, even four major literary novels every 24 hours – and not only that, but also deliver an acutely sensitive literary judgement on them live on Radio 4 before 10.00 p.m. the same day.

For this reason, I currently rank as one of the most sought-after literary jurists in this, or, indeed, any other, country. Over the past six months, I have been a judge of no less than eight separate literary prizes, for which I have been forced to read 272 works of non-fiction and 323 works of fiction – and this does not include poetry (576 poems in 3 weeks, including 3 epics, 14 elegies and 24 haikus) – for which prize money totalled £46,721.36, a free BA club class return to Los Angeles, a portable AppleMac, a complete set of Berol fibre-tip pens and a Rumbelows voucher exchangeable for £25.95 worth of electrical goods. Only last week, I was contacted by the organisers of the Booker Prize in the hope that I could squeeze in 157 new novels for a shortlist at the end of September. Meanwhile, I have had the privilege of serving as this year's joint Chair of the Orange Prize for Women's Fiction, selecting a shortlist of 20 novels by women from an initial entry of 224, and all in under 5 weeks 3 days 8 hours and 23 minutes.

This, I think you will agree, uniquely qualifies me to deliver an overview on current literary trends in the national and international arena, and my devastating *critiques* are taken with all due seriousness by senior news commentators, editors and literary experts. For the past few weeks, I have been happy to ghost-write the pronouncements of my good friend Professor Lisa Jardine, Lisa herself being tied up reading her way through the 112-strong shortlist for the new £43,000 Redhead Literary Prize for Fiction Written by Redheaded Women in New Zealand Between the Ages of 35 and 51, a prize that has met with a fair bit of controversy ever since top New Zealand woman novelist Keri Hulme was photographed by a security camera buying a bottle of henna in Auckland last week.

Personally, I am deeply – and sensitively – upset by the manner in which the British novel is growing increasingly parochial, sidelined on the world market by ambitious *international* novels written by *international* novelists who are not frightened to address wider issues, bigger issues, taller issues, longer issues – with no time at all for small or medium-sized issues, preferring extra-large issues for men and women, gentle, absorbent, kind to your senses and bonded and quilted for all-weather protection.

We need to expand our horizons. The British novel has become increasingly insular, dealing only with Britons in stories set more often than not in Britain, with few day trips to France, Holland or neighbouring countries. How much more fascinating is the work of, say, Canadian novelists, who set their works in foreign countries like, say, Canada or novelists from Greece, who are not content just to write about everyday family life in South-East London, choosing instead to take the bold, uncompromisingly ambitious decision to set their tales of everyday family life in the colourful, panoramic, distinctively *international* world of South-East Athens.

I like a new work of fiction to stop me in my tracks, to challenge and arrest me, and to carry conviction. Small wonder that British fiction down the centuries has made so little impact on the world stage. If only that consummate Little Englander Jane Austen had gone for the broader canvas, and had had the guts to let the plot of *Sense and Sensibility* sweep across 4 centuries and 6 continents, 8 time-zones and 10 narrative conventions, rather than confining it to the itsy-bitsy goings-on of a small toffee-nosed community somewhere boring in the Home Counties, then she might have succeeded in gaining a niche for herself in the world of international letters. And look at poor old Henry James: his characters just think and talk, talk and think, hardly ever meeting anyone beyond their own narrow social circle, rarely managing to nuance the complexities of their post-colonial sensibilities beyond the narrative constraints of their insular horizons.

We, too, need to enlarge our horizons. Our fiction must pay as much attention to the problems confronted by 5 generations of goat-farmers in Papua New Guinea as to the marital breakdown of a married couple in North London. We British have become too parochial, too insular, too turned in on ourselves. Shame on us! And one final plea: isn't it about time the Arts Council did something to promote the rebirth of the socially concerned novel tackling the problems faced by one-parent families in East Tyneside?

S is also for Shocking

the literally shattering legacy of dennis potter

Shattered. Literally shattered. That's how I felt after watching my first Dennis Potter play on television all those years ago. I forget its name, but it involved a naked blind girl being raped to the music of Fred Astaire and Ginger Rogers. Its effect was so overwhelming that when it was over I found it quite hard to concentrate on the repeat of *I Love Lucy* that followed, though after a reviving glass of dry white I sat back and enjoyed some bloody brilliant laughs with that lovely old stalwart of TV comedy.

'Bloody' – that's a word I couldn't have used in journalism before Dennis Potter came along. Now I can bloody well use it as much as I want. I find it places emphasis on the anger I feel at the way this world is going. And anger is an emotion Potter knew one helluva lot about.

As is well known, Potter started his career as a TV playwright writing episodes of *Dixon of Dock Green*. This provided excellent grounding for his subsequent career, teaching him structure and character development. 'Evenin' fuckin' all' begins the amiable George Dixon in Potter's first scripted episode for the series. Dixon then continues in his soft, avuncular voice: 'You know, folks, sometimes in a police force there crops up what we coppers call a "bad apple". Shifty types, without a shred of ordinary human honesty. You can spot 'em a mile off. Well, PC Arthur Bent was one such character. And blow me down if in his spare time, his hobby wasn't raping naked blind girls to the tunes of Fred Astaire and Ginger Rogers.'

Alas, this script proved so far ahead of its time that BBC bosses refused to let it be transmitted without massive changes. The Arthur Bent character was turned into a 'good apple' and given a fresh hobby – betting on the greyhounds. Ten years later Potter was able to use the germ of his brilliant idea in ten separate drama series – and to devastating effect.

After an unhappy time drafting unused scripts for the presenters of BBC/TV's *Blue Peter* programme ('This fuckin' balsa wood's bloody useless for makin' bleedin' traction engines,' says Christopher Trace at a crucial moment, to which the youthful Valerie Singleton replies simply but effectively, 'Shut your gob, arsehole.') Potter was moved sideways to the BBC Religious Affairs department. At first, he seemed ideally suited to scripting the links on the long-running *Songs of Praise*.

But here, too, there were undeniable hiccups. The first to make his objections plain was the Bishop of Leicester, the Rt. Rev. Roger Birtwhistle, who vehemently refused to introduce the well-loved family hymn 'All Things Bright and Beautiful' with Potter's scripted words 'Fuck this for a game of soldiers – all things grim and bloody terrible, more like', complaining in the typically bourgeois manner of the so-called Established Church that some viewers might be 'shocked and outraged' by such language.

'Nuff said. But of course the whole point of Potter lay in his ability to shock, to lift us as viewers out of our complacency. I'll never forget watching that bit in *The Singing Detective* where the blind girl is raped by her father while he mimes a cheerful medley of the music of Fred

Astaire and Ginger Rogers. Let me tell you this: never in my life had I been so shocked out of my complacency. I straightaway changed my ideas about everything I ever thought I knew. The very next morning I marched headlong into WH Smith in Sloane Square and ordered a double cassette of the songs of Fred Astaire and Ginger Rogers to play in my new car. I've been a lifelong Astaire/Rogers fan ever since. And I am not alone. The soundtrack reached number 8 in the charts, and stayed there for a full three weeks.

And his influence didn't end there. The minute I got out of WH Smith I rushed straight into the Garden Furnishings Department at The Conran Shop and ordered a ninety per cent Teak Four-Person Garden Bench, just like the one the blind girl had been lying on. That's the kind of effect Potter had on viewers. These days, whenever I feel an attack of complacency coming on, I slot *The Singing Detective* into the video. Within minutes, I am able to congratulate myself on shedding all the complacency I ever had.

It was typical of the man that he should broadcast his dying wishes to Melvyn on camera. First, he demanded that his final two plays be produced and broadcast jointly by BBC and Channel 4. Next he demanded – off camera, but no less forcefully – that BBC boss John Birt and Channel 4 boss Michael Grade set off together on a bicycling holiday in the New Forest on a tandem bought jointly by their two companies. He further insisted that the two should stop along the way and look at all the landmarks portrayed in Potter's shockingly memorable *Pennies from Heaven*, and that throughout their three-week trip they should wear Lycra cycling shorts purchased exclusively from Millets.

The two bosses were only too eager to comply with Potter's demands rather than be thought churlish. It was truly great to receive a chatty postcard from the two of them, sent from exactly the spot where the blind girl was raped to the music of Ginger Rogers and Fred Astaire in *Pennies from Heaven*. Potter was a visionary who despised more than anything the mute acceptance of dictatorial commands. It is up to all of us in the media to prove him right, and to do whatever he wanted.

S is also for Solidarity

melvyn, harriet: harriet, melvyn

Tony, Bel: Bel, Tony. Hi, Bel. Hi, Tony. How are you, Bel?
Fine, Tony. And you, Tony? Fine, Bel – have you met Harriet,
Bel? Bel, Harriet: Harriet, Bel.

Simple words cannot communicate the truly fantastic
memories I have of the first, very, very informal time I ever
met Tony Blair. The year was 1984, the occasion a special
fund-raising dinner at the River Café for the striking miners
of West Sussex. We were at a table of seven, the others being
Melvyn Bragg, who was producing a *South Bank Show* special
on the new movement in free-form mime and poetry among
the miners' wives of Chichester and surrounding areas,
Melvyn's hard-hitting nephew, Billy, who had recorded an
album, *Petsworth's Glory*, in praise of one of the worst-hit of
all the mining communities in the area, my good chum
Harriet Harman, who even at that early stage in her career
was already heavily politicised, wearing Estée Lauder jet-
black mascara and dark tights to show solidarity with the
striking miners of East Wittering, the super Barbara Follett,
who had a special sympathy with the Sussex miners as her
under-gardener's sister had once been married to
a Goodwood miner, and finally my then-companion, the
lovely Jack Straw, who had come out strongly and

unequivocally in favour of the striking miners, provided they kept their worries to themselves and didn't pester ordinary, decent citizens with requests to wash, polish or in any other way tidy up their vehicles.

It was a truly great evening. Each three-course dinner cost £30 a head, with a full 10% going to the striking miners of West Sussex, once service and cover charge had been deducted. Of course, Tony nearly put his foot in it just before the first course – Goat's Cheese and Polenta Mascarpone with Braised Fennel and Charred Cod's Skin on a Bed of Crispy Ox-Tongue with a Blackcurrant and Gingerbread Coulis – arrived. He had just got his serviette in place when he blurted out, 'To be honest, I didn't know there were any mines in West Sussex.'

'*To-neeee!*' I exclaimed. I couldn't believe the guy's ignorance. 'Of course there are no mines in West Sussex. That's why they're striking! They are victims of the iron heel of Thatcherism, failing to develop and expand natural resources in all areas of the country, forcing ordinary men and women to become computer programmers, dental technicians, merchant bankers, hospital administrators and stockbrokers rather than following their true calling to work down the mines of West Sussex.'

But we were all prepared to forgive such gaffes. And the reason? Two little words: first names.

'Melvyn: Harriet, Harriet: Melvyn. Jack: Melvyn, Melvyn: Jack. Jack: Billy, Billy: Jack. Billy: Barbara, Barbara: Billy. Barbara: Tony, Tony: Barbara. Tony: Bel, Bel: Tony . . .' First names lent us an instant rapport, an instant solidarity. If we were going to tackle the grave social problems facing a beleaguered nation over a three-course meal with wine and coffee, then we were bloody well going to need all the first names we could muster. Before long, we were singing along to Billy Bragg's moving, plangent chant: 'I stand by the miners of Billingshurst/And I fight with my fists and my teeth/'Cos I'm marchin' for freedom and liberty/From Bishop's Waltham to Haywards Heath.'

I may have been too hasty in rushing to condemn the shilly-shallying of the new government. Sorry, Tony! As we all know, Tony's taken the truly brave decision to use first names in Cabinet, signalling a new, informal, less dictatorial approach to government. And, by heavens, he really means it. He's made it clear that if anyone is caught using a surname or job-description, they'll be out.

No more stuffy, out-dated 'Good morning, Secretary of State for Foreign Affairs' or 'Good morning, Prime Minister and First Lord of the Treasury'. Now it's just 'Hi, Tony' and 'Hi, Robin'. It's so much more friendly, and saves plenty of time for the real business of the day: employing a full range of audio-visual aids to present government initiatives in an attractive, positive and accessible light.

And Tony's also insisting that when the time comes for any member of the Cabinet to resign, their letter of resignation must remain strictly informal. Peter M has already drafted a dummy resignation letter for future use by all Cabinet ministers. 'Dear Tony,' it begins, 'it's been really, really great serving under you. Loved every minute. Sorry I cocked it up! Typical!! I blame myself! Must go now. Ciao! With lots of love from SIGN YOUR NAME HERE. p.s. All the best to Cherie and the kids from me and the missus.'

Yup. We've come a long way from the cold, dark days of the formal, last-name Tory jackboot. To paraphrase Hartley Shawcross, we're the mateys now. Okay, Tony? Big Kiss. Bel. Love ya!

S is also for Stark Horror

tragicasting

Me? I'm delighted by the courageous move by the BBC to televise the tragic and untimely death of a cancer victim, albeit in a sensitive and relevant fashion.

When John Birt appointed me Chair of the BBC Human Outsource Unit, he empowered me to draw up a ten-point vector-plan to look into the whole issue of death-friendly programming. The very first TV death comes, I'm proud to say, as the direct result of our report. Scheduled tactically and above all sensitively, it could well overtake *Crimewatch UK* and even touch *Morse* in the ratings.

For some years, the Audience Response Unit at the BBC has reported that projects targeted towards untimely tragedies constitute a productive and accessible use of our broadcasting resource budget. For instance, when the Challenger Space Shuttle tragically exploded within seconds of lift-off, the ARU reported satisfaction ratings of up to ninety-five per cent with up-to-the-minute shots of not only the tragic explosion but the tragic faces of victims' families in the tragic aftermath. This excellent tragedy-related performance graph – equalled only by the 1992 extended Christmas edition of *Only Fools and Horses* – encouraged us to repeat this stimulating, challenging and highly relevant footage on every news bulletin for the next seven days, and once every ten days thereafter.

The success of our Challenger programming in an increasingly segmented marketplace has creative reverberations which we have always looked to prioritise when opportunity allows. When Promotions first suggested the orange World Balloon as an onrunning inter-programme motif for BBC/TV, my Human Outsource Unit came up with a very useful six-point plan: for maximum audience uptake the hot-air balloon should at some point explode – perhaps over a city-centre, ideally with a wide sociological and economic range of passengers on board. This would not only catch viewers' attention, challenge preconceptions and increase figures, it would demonstrate the Corporation's firm commitment to reflecting flexible life-and-death concerns in a viable ongoing unballoon situation.

Tragic victims of terrorism, tragic families caught on balconies in flaming high-rise buildings, tragic victims of floods, volcanoes, earthquakes and lone gunmen, tragic motorists trapped in pile-ups, tragic tots in famine zones: these are the very stuff of serious and committed television coverage – as well as being a second-to-none resource for highly professional programming.

And where Tragicasting is concerned, sheer professionalism is the key. At present, the Human Outsource Unit is auditioning the terminally ill for a series of Tragicast specials, so that the discerning viewer is given a ringside seat as and when the outsourcing of the patient occurs. Competitors are being asked to complete a ten-point self-assessment, covering everything from the temporality of their conditions (obviously the BBC cannot commit resources to a patient who lingers beyond the three-month filming schedule) to the lighting conditions in the ward concerned. Obviously, priority will be given to those with families willing to participate in programme publicity nearer the time of transmission: the usual round of Esther, Jimmy Young and the upmarket Sundays is vital to ensure maximum viewer input.

We're very, very excited to have made television history with this powerful and moving testament to the sheer COPY-EDITOR FILL IN POIGNANT WORD of death. But the BBC is not an organisation to rest on its laurels. I can today upfront my Unit's prediction that before the end of next year, a BBC crew will have accompanied its first corpse to its final resting-place, followed by sustained fly-on-the-coffin broadcasting charting the progress of the corpse over its first year of delayering and downsizing.

Future outsource plans also include mould-breaking live coverage of the execution of a tragic criminal in a Texas penitentiary. This hugely responsible programme – handled throughout with the full cooperation of the participant – will allow the viewer access to an essential feature of our existence. To avoid depicting the stark reality of this tragic event would be not only cowardly but wholly unprofessional. We confidently expect a broader viewer reach for these reinvigorated Tragicasts than for The Funeral of Diana or even *EastEnders*. And you can't argue with figures like that.

S is also for Sympathy

tall-poppy syndrome

Ouch. The Australians have a word for it. Tall-Poppy Syndrome. When a person gets to walk too tall, we cut them down to size. And that, I perceive, is what's happening to my good and valued friend Tony Blair.

He's a busy guy. Passing through Tel Aviv airport on Tuesday, he had to call an emergency press conference in order to pass on the Government's congratulations to the producers of *The Full Monty* for scooping the BAFTA awards. He'd barely embarked on his top-level talks with Binyamin Netanyahu when he was forced to excuse himself ('Look, I'm gonna have to ask you to schlepp it without me, okay, guys?') so as to issue a press statement commending the decision by Granada to grant an early release to Deirdre Rachid.

Another twenty minutes into his discussions with Mr Netanyahu and Tony was called out yet again, this time to make it clear he welcomed 'unequivocally' Grant Bovey's decision to return to his wife Della and their two young daughters, whilst offering his 'fullest sympathy' to the lovelorn Anthea Turner, pleading with the nation 'let's not take sides'. 'On a personal note,' he added in an unscripted aside, 'may I also mention that Ms Turner's estranged husband Peter Powell has acted with truly terrific dignity throughout his lengthy ordeal.'

And his sense of commitment to the British people didn't end there. On arrival in Egypt on the Wednesday, Tony called a press conference in the Cairo Hilton to combat rumours that he was indifferent to the separation between Mrs Anna Murdoch and her husband Rupert, 'a good friend to New Labour'. He took the opportunity to add that he was following the French inquiry into the death of Diana, Princess of Wales 'with keen interest', that his heart went out to the family of the ailing Frank Sinatra, that both he and his kids were enjoying the new CD by Simply Red, and that he welcomed the new park-and-ride scheme recently put into operation by Chester City Council.

Just two short hours later, his office had issued a statement from Tony confirming that he would be wearing a short-sleeved Royal blue aertex shirt while kicking a ball about with the kids this weekend, weather permitting, and adding that 'the Prime Minister has sent a handwritten message of deep-felt sympathy to Mr Dustin Hoffman on the conviction of his adopted daughter on a charge of embezzlement.'

A busy guy doing one helluva busy job. About time someone gave him a break, you might think. Wrong again. Suddenly, whaddyaknow, Tall Poppy Syndrome sets in. Tony had barely regained his breath after a press conference in Abu Dhabi, stressing his government's abiding enthusiasm for the new-look Radio 4, when he was attacked for letting a tiny little bit of radioactive uranium into this country. Yet his critics seem unaware, bless 'em, that this policy is entirely in tune with Tony's longstanding commitment to increasing job opportunities in the Scottish Health Sector.

My own commitment to Green issues is not in question. As an award-winning columnist, my opinions – many of them recycled under licence to the Scott Trust – have put me at the forefront of the Green campaign. With Anita Roddick, I spent three months in 1985 introducing Peppermint and

Avocado Foot-Lotion to the Iriqoi Rainforest Tribesmen of New Mexico, so don't lecture me on environmental awareness, thank you very much.

It's already been announced that my award-winning Public Relations agency, Bel & Frendz, long-time specialists in Green matters, has accepted the Government account for a new 'Let's Go Fission!' Uranium promotion, designed to increase public awareness of the positive aspects of this attractive yet alluringly volatile element. In June, we launch a Cool Uranium celebration, in which the very best of British fashion designers are given their chance to show uranium-based costumes in a gorgeous explosion of pinks, greens and oranges. In August, Peter M will be announcing the new Uranium Zone in the Millennium Dome Experience, letting visitors experience all the creative excitement of radioactivity for themselves, so that kids and adults alike will emerge from the Zone positively humming and buzzing with reaction. Go, Uranium, Go! Obviously, Tony would have told you all this himself, only he was having to issue bulletins saying how much he was enjoying the new Nick Hornby.

T is for Thinky-Wordy-Lifestyley-Serialkillery

betcha-by-golly-wow!

The most happening initials in the world today? TB.

TB stands not just for Tony B – though that's quite good enough for me! – but also for his close friend and important contact Tina Brown, now celebrating her fifth year as world-famous editor of the legendary *New Yorker*.

In that time, she's turned the magazine round from being, in her own words, a stodgy literary-thinky-snorey kinda thing to being a prestigious sensibility-sell lifestyle arts-stroke-pulsetaking niche magazine alive with the latest literary gossip, high fashion and top-rating murder – as well as boasting high-precision wordy-wordy pieces from some of the most costly writers in the world and a running loss of an impressive $1 million a month.

As the *New Yorker*'s Special European Projects Editor with Coordinating Responsibility for Homicide and Haute Couture, I have grown to admire Tina's tremendous sense of energy and style. She really knows how to turn a piece round, so that if a kind of thinky-classy Saul Bellowy kind of subordinate-clausey kinda writer hands in what we call a writey-writey piece on, say, 'The Novel in the 21st Century', and we're all, like, thinking 'Whadda we gonna do with *that*?', then Tina will be able to take one look at it and after barely a glance she'll say, 'Didn't Karla-Faye Tucker have something to say about the novel in the 21st century before the fatal and tragic needles plunged into her arms in three different places? I want it on my desk by lunchtime – and let's get Bellow dressed by Givenchy for a beautiful black and white portrait, maybe in a captain's hat so it has a tribute-to-the-*Titanic*-Leonardo-di-Caprio style feel to it – I want Helmut Newton on the line *now*!' That may well turn what would have been a kinda special-interest EngyLitty kinda brainbox-cum-swotty piece into an ohmygod-must-read-this kinda piece. And, believe me, with no overall loss to the Big Q: Quolity.

You see, The *New Yorker* is a quolity-led magazine, so Tina's always keen to surround herself with max-quolity-type-people, well-dressed, well-read, well-connected. And she wants her max-quol people to surround themselves with max-quol people too: she has that caring thing about her. So, like, three months ago, she faxed me and around two hundred, two hundred and fifty very, very close friends, saying the White House had specifically asked her for information input on potential-invitee A-listy kinda people to last week's White House Ball in honour of Cherie and Tony, so she was resourcing mutual colleagues for feedback-style in-flow possibilities as to who Cherie and Tony's contacts-stroke-friend-type-contacts might be, either now or in the future, but let's forget the past, okay?

Tina makes no bones about being a New Laboury lady to the core. Don't talk to her about the downtrodden in our society: half of them are in her office. And *New Yorker* magazine has the most fabulous social conscience. Our editors are always on the look-out for ten- or even twelve-thousand word takes on say, transsexual victims of serial murderers, however lowly they may be, or, like, date-rape ex-girlfriends of the Kennedys, or Miami low-lifers who once sustained intimacy with Gianni Versace, or tragic, tragic, photogenic-style kids like Jon-Benet Ramsey or alternatively very, very moving and humane-type exclusive coma-style photographs of Sunny Von Bulow in hospital, maybe dressed by Calvin Klein. Her social reach is that wide, that compassionate, that real, that beautiful.

To me, Tina's a warrior for truth. If she wants to know the truth about what's going on in the White House, she's not gonna bother with no underdog, she's not gonna sully her hands with the used goods, hell no, she's gonna go straight to the President himself, or at very least to his Chief of Staff, and she's gonna say, hey, forget the squalor and rancour of the trivia corps, I want the truth and I want it now, how about, like, your press guys come right out with it and say the President didn't know nothing and we print it over five, six thousand words – could we move a deal where we get exclusive rights to a full-colour photograph of the President and Hillary maybe dancing on the White House lawn, their love and mutual respect boundless, the President looking absurdly debonair, his blue, blue eyes projecting a kind of avid inclusiveness that encircles every jaded celebrity they honour with their touch?

And one TB just adores the other TB. Tony Blair is to her not just the kinda guy who knighted Elton John, not just the kinda guy who made it from nowhere to the top of the Britcool tree, not just the kinda guy whose wife still shoots him that ardent look that says, 'Darling, we made it, didn't we?' No, sirree, Tony's also the kinda guy who can help Tina help others help Tina. As they say in the States, with all their contagious enthusiasm and superb lack of cynicism, 'Betcha-by-golly-wow!' And that just about says it all.

T is also for Touched by Genius

the queen of the safety-pin

Great to see Vivienne Westwood getting some hard-won recognition at last. Why is it we spare so little time praising our home-grown fashion designers? Besides tossing Vivienne an OBE, twice awarding her Designer of the Year, and very, very occasionally permitting her on TV and radio (she wasn't on last week at all, and only twice the week before) we otherwise totally ignore her.

Have you noticed how Westwood is confined to the fashion and feature pages? Yet there is so much that is overtly *political* in her work, it should by rights be featured in the news and politics pages, alongside Helmut Kohl, Saddam Hussein, Jack Straw and President Clinton. *Example*: in 1989, when the Berlin Wall came down, Vivienne celebrated the event with her brilliant Honecker Collection, in which international models paraded on the catwalks wearing male suits influenced by the retired East German leader Eric Honecker, but with the material around the buttocks missing. 'For me, the fabric around the buttocks represents the Berlin Wall – unduly constricting to personal freedom,' philosophised Vivienne on *Start the Week*, 'so I've pulled it right down, and now the buttocks are celebrating their new-found freedom. And it's only £899.99 including VAT.'

Ever since the seventies, her influence on fashion and popular culture has been all-pervasive. There is literally no one in public life whose style hasn't been touched by her genius. Take the Royal Family, for instance. Throughout the sixties and seventies, the Queen eschewed see-through mauve velour tank-tops with one breast exposed to the air. Some will say she still does, but – believe me – that tells you more about the British Establishment than it does about Vivienne Westwood. And I have it on good authority that the Queen Mother's recent hip-replacement surgery came about after she had been strutting around Clarence House in Viv's eight-inch sawn-off heels, only to come a cropper on the over-polished parquet of the State Dining Hall. And as Style Consultant to the Princess of Wales, I was always strongly encouraging Diana to wear more and more Westwood. 'You want the public to feel sorry for you,' I would explain.

Ever since the seventies, Vivienne has remained at the forefront of the social revolution. Sid Vicious, Johnny Rotten and whatever the other two Sex Pistols were called – these names are now immortal. It was in 1976, operating from a small shop on the King's Road, with no more than a set of bicycle chains and a couple of safety-pins to her name, that Vivienne vowed to change society forever. A few weeks later, Harold Wilson made his surprise decision to quit Number 10, and on the very same day Lord Snowdon and Princess Margaret announced that they were to separate. The Westwood Revolution had begun.

The death of Chairman Mao followed four months later. He was pictured lying in state wearing a distinctive Westwood 'Mao' Jacket. Such was the nature of Vivienne's growing international reputation that literally millions of ordinary Chinese queued for hours in Tiananmen Square simply to catch a glimpse of it. Other Westwood-inspired events were to follow: the election of Margaret Thatcher, the fall of the Shah (the Ayatollah was always very influenced by Westwood, though his long beard often hid his jewel-encrusted plunge-neck bustier from public view), and the economic growth of the Pacific Rim among them.

Just as Vivienne had redefined the '70s, so she now set about inventing the '80s. Her appeal was always rooted in a passionate quest to create the unexpected, using fine art, philosophy and literature as her inspiration. She rarely went anywhere without a book, and in 1981 she redesigned her famous platform heels to incorporate a small pocket library of the *Complete Works of William Shakespeare*. From the world of philosophy, there was no one she admired more than Montaigne, though she had reservations about his eveningwear collection.

And now Viv is to become the official standard-bearer of the Blair Revolution. Introduced to the Party by her friend Barbara Follett, she has set about breathing new life into New Labour, and her Spring 'Stakeholder' Collection is already catching on throughout the country, each design based on the ethos surrounding a key New Labour politician. Already street-wise kids are donning Westwood-designed clip-on red beards and crumpled brows in pursuit of this season's Robin Cook Look, and Oxford Street shops are reporting a run on the Jack Straw Leisurewear Collection.

Where next for this wayward genius? She has already revolutionised the way we see fashion. Never again will we be able to look at a £1,200 price tag on a ruched skirt and think that it's just for the very rich. No, the pricing's all an essential part of the subversive humour that makes such a classic British designer. Hail Genius! Hail Vivienne!

T is also for Tears

a kettle from rumbelows

Okay, so we've got a New Labour Government, and that's great, but there's still a lot of terrible, terrible things going on in this world of ours. Only recently, a good friend of mine bought a new cordless telephone set in which the batteries were not included. And there's worse.

I'm talking Consumer Problems. And I make no apology if the tale I have to tell brings tears to your eyes.

In October of this year, Ms Pauline Sparks of Runcorn bought a new kettle from her local branch of Rumbelows. All went well until 11.15 a.m. on 3 November. Feeling like a refreshing pick-me-up cup of decaffeinated coffee, Ms Sparks pressed the prominently displayed 'ON' switch of her new kettle and waited for it to boil. She then poured the water into a mug containing a teaspoon of decaffeinated coffee granules. She subsequently added one heaped teaspoon of sugar and the equivalent of two tablespoons of milk. Ms Sparks was all set to enjoy a well-earned cup of coffee when disaster struck.

The telephone rang unexpectedly; leaning over to answer it, Ms Sparks inadvertently struck the edge of her coffee cup with a loose bit of cardigan hanging from her left elbow. This caused the cup's contents to spill over a freshly laundered cotton tablecloth which she had purchased only three months before in an August sale at her local Debenhams. Despite repeated visits to her laundry, the coffee-stains have remained on the tablecloth in question ever since.

Ms Sparks first reaction was to take the cotton tablecloth back to her local Debenhams. But, after repeated inquiries, the store's Consumer Complaints officer informed her that as they had at no time advertised the tablecloth in question as stainproof, there was nothing they could do about it. This prompted Ms Sparks to take her problem to The Spring Clothing Company, manufacturers of the cardigan that had proved so loose-fitting that she had brushed the coffee cup against it, causing the spillage. But the company denied all responsibility. 'Once the garment is purchased,' an official informed her, 'it becomes the responsibility of the wearer. We cannot legally be held to account for any damage or loss thereby incurred.'

At this point, Ms Sparks could have been forgiven for imagining she was the fly caught in the centre of a web of British retail manufacturers. Bravely, she decided to go it alone. Her next stop? Zurich, the international headquarters of the coffee manufacturers Nescafé. Why, she asked the Chairman, had they not made it clear on the label that their instant decaffeinated coffee contained a staining agent, and why was there no clear warning? The Chairman put her in touch with Nescafé's Consumer Affairs spokesperson, who took over three days to reply: the company could bear no responsibility for the stains.

But Ms Sparks was not to be outdone by the Fat Cats of consumer durables. By now, she had given up a highly paid job as well as sacrificing her home and her family in order to gain justice for herself and others like her. She immediately despatched a letter to the head of Zanussi, the Tokyo-based company that manufactured the kettle, asking him what he planned to do about the stains on her tablecloth. She sent a copy of this letter to the head office of Rumbelows, adding a handwritten postscript alerting them to the fact that they were stocking a faulty line, and suggesting an immediate withdrawal of any remaining kettles before further table-cloths were ruined. Two months have gone by, and Ms Sparks is still waiting for a reply. From Rumbelows, she received a curt letter, stating that – and I quote – 'as you will appreciate, we are unable to offer you the free set of table-linen, the new kettle and the automatic fridge-freezer you suggest. Thank you for your inquiry.' Only yesterday, Ms Sparks sent further missives to British Telecom, asking them to compensate her for problems caused by the unexpected phone-call, and to the local pottery from which she had purchased the coffee cup in question, calling into question the stability of their produce.

I make no apology for devoting valuable space to this devastating tale. Even my colleague Paul Foot, with his wide experience of miscarriages of justice, will be taken aback by the fate of Pauline Sparks. And that's where I come in. As the new presenter of *You and Yours*, the long-running consumer programme on BBC Radio 4, I am in a position to right these grave wrongs.

Over the course of the series, I will be using my position to cross-question senior representatives of the companies involved. Soon, I'll be putting it to Mr L. Griffith, Customer Relations Officer of Debenhams, that there should be immedi-ate legislation – provisionally titled The Hot Beverages on Cotton Tablecloths Bill – to safeguard the statutory rights of all those who find their new tablecloths irreparably damaged by hot beverages. And I'll also be hauling ministers over the coals. Henceforth, I will be calling for eighteen different additions to current legislation to safeguard not only our households but our basic liberties. If you, too, have encountered a problem that requires further legislation, do please write to me, Bel Littlejohn, c/o *You and Yours*. Together, we can get things banned.

U is for Uptight

ooh, i can fly like a bluebird in the sky

In this business, you can't stick your head out, week after week, and expect to have an easy time of it. But I've never been afraid to speak out on issues that truly concern me. Why be an award-wining opinion-former, if not to shake up society, even if it means getting shot down in the process? And that's why you'll always spot the name Littlejohn, Bel between Lane, Carla, and Mansfield, Michael, QC, on letters to editors from the most distinguished and caring men and women of our generation.

A glimpse through my cuttings-book tells me that so far this year I've been brave enough to add my name to over thirty-five such petitions, ranging from a letter to *The Times* (fellow signatories Arnold Wesker and Imogen Stubbs – well done, both – and thanx!) in which we retrospectively called on President Johnson for an end to the war in Vietnam, and a letter to the *Guardian* (fellow signatories Billy Bragg and Polly Toynbee) voicing our concern with this government's decision to go ahead regardless.

Yes, it's been tough and occasionally terrifying, but I've survived – just! This week I couldn't be prevented from adding my name to a petition that means more to me than any other. I'm talking, of course, about the *Independent on*

Sunday's brave and long-overdue campaign to decriminalise cannabis. 'We the undersigned,' it begins, 'are totally freaked out by the way the pigs continue to get heavy with heads like us who just wanna have a really great time, right, and it's not hurting anyone else, is it? Or did I just say that?' Two hundred and fifty words later ('. . . We call on the Home Secretary to stop being so totally uptight . . .') comes an array of pretty well unknown names before, at last, you get to my own. Personally, if I'd been organising it, I'd've placed my own name, as a so-called 'celebrity', right at the top, but there we are.

Memories, memories. It may cause me to face physical retribution from the fuzz and possible prosecution, but what the hell – I'm going to come out into the open right now and recall my first joint. It was 1967, I was at Leeds University, I had just come back from a truly awesome Edgar Broughton concert, some guy offered me a toke, the next thing I knew I had eaten six Chicken Biryanis, three Sag Bhajis, a dozen poppadoms and a small vase of carnations – and I was still only halfway through trying to tell everyone about this amazing dream I had where this massive great sort of thing was kind of coming towards me like something out of, well, a dream.

From that point on, I never looked back, and though for personal reasons I haven't had any dope for twenty-five years, I still care passionately about it, regardless of whether they lock me up. Courage, Bel, courage.

This historic petition is more than just a start. Faced with powerful names like PR supremo Lynne Franks, author Tim Madge, Liberal Democrat MP Donald Gorrie, Geoff Baker (publicist to Paul and Linda McCartney) and Ron Smedley (medical receptionist) it can't be long before the authorities are forced to give way on this important issue. Personally, I've been making my outspoken views known to my high-level contacts in the Government – with results that are totally mindblowing.

Over dinner with senior government ministers on

Wednesday, I offered round a kiwi torte from the *River Café Cookbook*, with a good bit of dope added, just like in the old days. I'm not going to name those ministers in print – let's just call them Jack S, Harriet H, Peter M and Gordon B – but the effect was positively electric.

Gordon B, usually so reserved, stopped talking about interest rates and began staring avidly at his spoon. 'Hey! You guys!' he said. 'I can see my reflection in this spoon – only I'm upside down!' He then waved the spoon in the air, following it with his eyes as it swooped back and forth, back and forth. 'Oooh, I can fly!' he said, and suddenly he began tapping his toes and clicking his fingers. 'Like a bluebird in the sky!'

'Six o'clock alarm would never ring!' joined in Harriet H, stretching out her arms and twirling her forefingers in the air in time with the beat.

And then Peter M, who up until then had been quietly perusing the site-plan for the Millennium Dome, tore off his tie, ripped off his shirt and bellowed, 'Cheer up, sleepy Jean, oh, what can it mean, for a –'

'DAYDREAM BELIEVER!' we all chorused, and at that very moment Jack S leant over to Peter M, pulled away his site-plan for the Millennium Dome, tore it it into the shape of a paper hat, and carried on singing, 'And a homecoming quee-eee-eee-een!'

Politically, it was a momentous night. As we polished off our eighth vindaloo, Jack S decided not only that he was with the squeegee merchants all the way, but that he was personally going to pay them to soap him all over, Gordon B announced that in future his fiscal policy was going to be fuelled by love, love, love, Peter M said that from now on it wasn't going to be a Dome at all, but a shiny golden sphere, sailing high in the clouds like a sort of psychedelic octopus, and Harriet H said nothing at all but just smiled and smiled. A watershed evening, then, for this government, and for our campaign. But who'll tell Tony?

151

V is for Vengeance

he done her wong

Crusader for truth, my foot. Don't talk to me about Jonathan Aitken. We at the *Guardian*, bless us, have had him up to here. As each day goes by, we accumulate more details of his perfidy. Soon we will be forced to publish a daily tabloid section devoted entirely to outlining his foibles, indiscretions and fibs. Public humiliation, a bill of millions of pounds, a ruinous divorce settlement and the stripping of his Privy Councillorship are too good for the beast. His expensive Savile Row suits should be shredded and the doors of his snooty Lord North Street house thrown open to a theatre workshop. And what about the man himself? Surely all reasonable, fair-minded liberal humanists with an ounce of compassion in their hearts must have come to the conclusion that Aitken has been humiliated enough: now he should be thrown into prison and clinically castrated (under controlled medical supervision, employing an effective but inexpensive anaesthetic).

I can now reveal that I am working on a biography of Jonathan Aitken. I have unearthed several more facts about the man's early life that I consider truly shocking. I'm sorry, but I do.

Aged just seven years old, engaging in a game of Junior

Scrabble against his sister Maria, the young Aitken attempted to persuade her that the word 'pilot' was spelt 'pilert' – thus ensuring himself a double word score. Subsequent perusal of the *Shorter Oxford English Dictionary* convinced his contemporaries that Aitken had been culpable of grave deceit. *Mysteriously, the police were never called in to investigate the charge.* Already, it seems, young Jonathan had friends in high places.

At the age of nine, Aitken won four shillings and sixpence on the coconut shy at a local fun-fair. Forty years on, my researchers have spent months trying to trace those coconuts to test them for tell-tale signs of oiling. *But they have been unable to trace them.* This suggests that, realising his bluff was about to be called, Aitken has used his position as an ex-MP and multi-millionaire to have the coconuts spirited away to a top-secret hide-out in Mexico, Malaysia or Saudi Arabia.

Comfortable among the toffee-nosed set at Eton School, Aitken sat a major exam. It was while taking this exam that, flying in the face of every known rule, the young Aitken *wrote on both sides of the paper.* Nevertheless, he passed the exam. A case of using his high-flown contacts to bribe the examiners? We shall never know – the only examiner we were able to trace died mysteriously over ten years ago – *even though he was a comparatively young octogenarian.*

Aged twenty-one, the dashing young Aitken was spotted by a contemporary talking to an attractive young lady. The contemporary clearly remembers Aitken saying, 'I'll just go and get a drink but I'll be right back.' Aitken was observed heading for the drinks' table. He was then spotted with a drink in his hand *talking to someone else entirely.* It is not known whether the attractive young lady then broke down in tears, or whether she ever recovered from this merciless act of cruelty to lead a normal, healthy life. But associates recoil when describing the way in which, when challenged over this incident, Aitken merely replied – coldly and flinty eyed – that he had 'no memory of it at all'.

So much for the young Jonathan, bounder, cad, rogue, villain and friend of foreigners. But there is one wholly unforgivable crime the older Jonathan perpetrated, one crime alone that was to condemn him in the eyes of right-minded folk.

He made Carol Thatcher cry.

How could he have done it? I mean, how could he? How could a grown man – a church-goer, for what it's worth – cause tears to course down the cheeks of the blameless Carol Thatcher by denying her the right to marry him? The image haunts me. I'm sorry, but I can't get it out of my mind. Sometimes I wake in the middle of the night, pouring with sweat, dreaming I am Carol Thatcher and I am in Lord North Street and Jonathan Aitken is casting me to one side like a piece of used Elastoplast and the tears are streaming down my face and I am horribly unhappy and I am shouting 'Mummy! Mummy! Mummy! HE DONE ME WONG!' It's an upsetting image, an image no woman can forgive, an image that should be engraved on Aitken's cold, cold heart for ever. In fact, I would urge the courts to further punish the brutal Aitken by forcing him, under medical supervision, to undergo the tattooist's drill. A picture of the weeping Carol branded on Aitken's forehead in vivid reds, blues and oranges would send a beacon to the world, and no woman would ever again fall for his diabolic charms.

As I say, we've all had about as much as we can stomach of Mr so-called Aitken. Arms dealing? Count me out! As we pore over the Aitken dossier, those of us who live decent lives, lives free from dinners with dusky Arabs in five-star foreign hotels, free from kinky sex-romps and far too much money, should take pride in our achievements. Personally, I award myself a great big pat on the back whenever I read about Aitken, and I advise you to do the same. There's nothing like one rotten apple in the barrel to make the rest of us feel better. Aitken! Aitken! Aitken! Out! Out! Out!

V is also for Vibrant

understatement is back with a vengeance

Paris. Beige is the new black and maroon is the new turquoise – this year's Paris shows have taught us that much.

The '30s are definitely back – but now underpinned by a very postmodern genuflection to the '40s, tinged with the spirit of the '50s, but with more than a hint of the '70s and a characteristically audacious touch of the '80s. This makes it one of the most '20s shows ever to have been staged so far in the '90s.

Elbows are back in a big way, and so too are vertebrae, nostrils and that part of the body on the reverse side of the leg from the knee which doesn't really have a name but which Ally Capellino has been celebrating this year in beautiful flowing greens and purples.

Understatement is back with a vengeance: bold, brazen and totally knockout. Top designer Mirman took understatement to dazzling new extremes when, in a witty postmodern move that was to make their fashion house the envy of all, top supermodel Stella Tennant never actually appeared on stage. Instead, a press release revealed that she was wearing a brand-new top-secret Mirman chunky mohair two-piece in a secure hideaway somewhere in Brazil: rarely has the fashion world been so excited by such sheer stylish self-effacement, and the buzz has it that invisible orders from top fashion buyers are already pouring in.

Bacon is back in a big way, both the painter and the pork cut. The legacy of Francis Bacon was conjured up by the genius of Giorgio Armani in his new 'Screaming Popes' collection: his models arrived on the catwalk immaculately dressed in purples and whites as Pope Innocent X, screaming in a silent world of horror, panic and revulsion – an absolute must for the beach this summer.

Both streaky and smoked back bacon were prominently on display in the Issey Miyake show, which was staged this year in a leading Left Bank abattoir. Particularly impressive were the all-Danish hats, not to mention the sizzling one-piece, lightly turned and with edges specially burnt. The effervescent Pork Scratchings Collection, with a very special crinkly cut, had a salty, hard-bitten, exquisitely trotterish feel to it.

There is always a healthy dose of wit to be found in the collections of Alexander McQueen, who has transformed the house of Givenchy with at least two really good belly laughs this season. His signature laddered tights are still there, of course, but now they are worn over the head: wearers are advised to avoid banks, supermarkets, cash-points and all the major airlines. For McQueen, shoes are the new gloves: top supermodel Kate Moss wore a superb pair of matt-black spike-heeled loafers on her hands to great acclaim: the applause faltered only slightly when she took a tumble on the catwalk when it proved too slippery underfoot for her calfskin gloves.

Postmodernism is undoubtedly the new deconstruc-tionism whenever top intellectual menswear designers Vic and Ken Stein hit town. They acknowledge a major debt to Bertrand Russell in this season's new slink-knit Peruvian peasant jumpers: their catwalk models all puffed on pipes, their marvellously brushed-back hair white and bushy. And did I detect a hint of Friedrich Nietzsche in his sky-blue polo-necks? There was something about the cut of the shoulder to suggest that in the senseless turnover that is nature, man's Apollonian faculty inevitably builds images of the eternal to provide him with some form of solace. Impressive from a deconstructionist angle, too, were his sheer-cut denim Y-fronts, though Derrida may have baulked, or, indeed, bulked, at the elasticated waistband, which seems to offer an illusion of creative unity in a garment whose meaning must ultimately prove indeterminable.

Blue was the new mauve and expensive was the new cheap in Karl Lagerfeld's literally stunning new collection. Lagerfeld has always been heavily influenced by 1930s Berlin, but there is a strong feel, too, of 1970s Birmingham, with here and there a definite touch of Crossroads motel, with a bold, inventive use of Benny-hats, and collar-styling that serves as a tribute to motel under-manager David Hunter. But Lagerfeld's philosophy remains centred on the thing he loves most: hard cash. 'My new Young Lagerfeld collection is above all an expression of my fundamental belief in my passion for my spirit in searching for an expression of my fundamental belief,' he says in his press release, 'but until I find what I am looking for, cash will do very nicely, thank you.'

So far, the great British success has been Vivienne Westwood's new collection 'Crumbs and Punishment', which was heavily influenced by both Dostoyevsky and Huntley and Palmer. Staged in La Bastille, it kicked off to a powerful start with top supermodel Jerry Hall as an elderly lady clubbed to death with a selection of sponge fingers. The rest of the show had a very strong biscuity taste to it, combined with a pervading sense of doom: gorgeous chiffon wraparound combat pants with a walnut centre were worn with a funeral director's coat – perfect for that mid-summer chocolate bourbon party or for balmy nights down the local pawnbrokers.

Cool Britannia was reflected in the new Prescott look premiered by leading menswear designer Paul Smith: baggy double-breasted suits in brave off-grey worn just above the stomach, pre-drenched by hand in Britpop wines and spirits by leading figures in the music scene. British stars were out in force for the Paul Smith show: front-seat positions were held by up-and-coming *Titanic* star Steve Brown (nineteenth corpse from the right, second shot from last) and his current date, glamorous longstanding *Emmerdale* pin-up no name supplied in press release.

Perhaps most daring of all was the Helen Highwater show. Highwater went for a revolutionary combination of comfort and elegance. Bizarrely, her models all appeared on the catwalk with their breasts and bottoms fully covered; one or two even managed a smile. The audience was aghast at such audacity, and even more astonished when it was revealed that – even more daringly – the clothes would remain intact after three or even four wears. Could this be the end of fashion as we know it?

W is for warmth

balewatch

At last, the Beeb (I always call it the Beeb – I'm not overawed by it, and I'm a much-loved regular in its corridors) has taken a brave decision. I'm talking, of course, of this week's move by Auntie (and I also often call the Beeb 'Auntie', just to show that I still regard her, ever so affectionately, as a bit of an old dinosaur) to acquit Esther of all charges brought against her and her lovely new show, *The Rantzen Report*. What's more, they've decided to award her a brand-new two-year contract, and that can't be bad.

Esther's come in for a lot of criticism these past few months. Call it off, guys: Esther's bigger than the lot of you. Ever since we first met, Esther's always hated bullies. Often I've seen her pick out a salesman she suspected of bullying a consumer and point an accusing finger at him, jab him in the chest, reduce him to a gibbering wreck, and ruin his sales career by naming him on live television. Then, wiping away his tears – and this is where her Heart of Gold comes in – she'll give him a bit of a cuddle, ask after his kiddies and cheer him up with an hilarious true story about a Garden Supplies Dealer from Droitwich who rejoices in the name of – can you believe it? – Mr Robert BENCH!!!

Esther and I were both educated at the University of Hard

Knocks. I first met her when we were working as researchers together on a pioneering documentary in the late '60s exposing the way a particular high-street department store preyed on its customers. Even though these customers included a lot of senior citizens, half of them on below-average income, a great many probably with debilitating diseases the medical profession still refuses to recognise, the store still continued to set out its wares all over its public 'showrooms', unfairly inducing its customers to crave goods many of them could not hope to buy.

Esther and I set out to teach ordinary decent folk to beware of unscrupulous tricks employed by the high-street manipulators, including:

• Some stores 'light up' their front windows at night, hoping to lure in the unsuspecting customer the next day.
• Expensive luxury items such as soft furnishings and electrical goods are covered in attractive colours and patterns – this encourages the unwary customer to be duped into buying them.
• In the lifts of many unscrupulous department stores, the various items on sale – ladies' fashions, records, household goods, etc. – are listed above the lift buttons. This is an obvious attempt by the heartless store-owners to fool the consumer into viewing – and possibly purchasing – many items he or she would not otherwise have considered.

Pretty shocking, eh? That's what we thought. Yet even after our hard-hitting series *Shopwatch*, successive governments have dragged their heels over the urgent legislation needed to ban store windows being lit at night, lists of items in store lifts and attractive coverings for sofas and armchairs.

But at least Esther and I became firm friends, and firm friends we remain. We both share a terrific sense of humour: in those far-off days of our youth we spent many a long hot summer fumbling through fields in search of root veg shaped like the male member. The minute we found one, we'd just sit down in the middle of the field and laugh and laugh and laugh. But before long our grins would turn to grimaces as we recalled what terrible things had happened to defenceless little mites as a result of real live men.

It was while leaving one of these fields one day that I fell over a discarded hay-bale by mistake, bruising the second finger along on my left hand. Frankly, Esther was in no mood to take my fall lying down, and she was never to forgive or forget that misplaced bale. Five years later, on her award-winning *That's Life*, she successfully campaigned for a special Balewatch helpline, advising viewers to report any stray bales in total anonymity. 'Our research proves con-clusively,' said Esther, 'that the apparently oh-so-harmless bale of hay can become a potential death-trap when strapped to the back of an innocent kiddie and set on fire.'

She then called for an all-out government ban on hay-bales, and adopting her most serious expression yet, added: 'Until legislation comes, our children will wander the countryside in mortal peril. Cyril?' And then the inimitable Cyril Fletcher entertained us all with one of his immortal 'Odd Odes'.

Since then, we've worked together on *Holidaywatch*, a pioneering programme that alerted unsuspecting consumers to the perils of foreign travel and called for urgent EU legislation to ensure that all buildings over 100 years old be fitted with adequate children's amusements, TV and light refreshments. Valuable, valuable work by a valuable, valu-able person. Welcome back, Esther, love.

W is also for Wanting Out

chinless wonders have no ears

She was a woman. A woman like me. And a woman like you. Unless you're a man, in which case, look, just forget about it, okay?

This is something a lot of people forget about Diana: her womanliness. There was nothing mannish about her, nothing at all. Nothing of the Paul Gascoigne, no hint of the Trevor McDonald or the Peter Hall. She had no use for staying up late playing football and belching and eating kebabs. She felt no need to wear thick-rimmed glasses or to read the News at Ten. And why should she be bothered to grow a goatee beard and direct yet another version of *Henry IV, Part 1* at the Old Vic? Not for Diana the emotionally cold life of the typical English male. There must have been literally hundreds of thousands of photographs taken of her during her life as a Princess, but never once was she photographed arm-wrestling her children, or strangling rabbits, or taking snuff, or any of those other strange, warped things English men get up to when no one else is around.

So she was, above all, a woman – this is the central thesis of my forthcoming work *Diana, Princess of Megastar*, soon to be published to great acclaim. And there was one other woman alive during the 1980s: Madonna. The parallels between Diana and Madonna were, indeed, extraordinary. Both had blond hair. Both liked buying clothes. Both were roughly the same height, give or take an inch or two. And both came from New York, except Diana, who came from England.

Diana was the first ever royal pop icon. Princess Anne never cut a record, never hand-jived to the Blow Monkeys at the Icebox. The Queen Mother never went ape-shit for the latest CD by Run DMC. But that was Diana through and through: she was the first pop star in the history of the world who managed to get to number one without ever releasing a record. Or she could have been, if she'd wanted to. But she didn't need to. She had nothing to prove. She was our first working-class Princess – and that was good enough for her.

It took Marilyn Monroe three marriages, fifteen movies and half a dozen nudie calendars to reach her level of fame. But it took Diana just a second – the time it takes to stammer 'yes' to the offer of marriage from an emotionally twisted Prince whose idea of a good time is to wade waist-deep in mud through the grouse-moors of Balmoral before going home to an ice-cold room to play a silent game of bridge with a livid, barbecuing, control-freak father, a thick-necked, toothy, weirdo naval brother and a grandmother from hell who spends her days swigging from a bottle of gin and hurling drunken abuse at her in-house greyhound tipsters.

But as her gold carriage sped its way back down the Mall after their goldfish-bowl marriage in St Paul's, Diana took one look at her new hubbie, his mouth creased in a rictus of self-loathing, his hands stealthily shuffling through saucy snapshots of his old flame, Mrs Parker-Bowles. At that moment she knew she wanted out – and wanted it real bad.

Okay, so her mouth stayed shut in that carriage – but her eyes spoke volumes. And the women of the world looking pitifully on could hear what they said. 'I know he doesn't love me,' said those eyes, as big as the moon, but not yet landed on by Neil Armstrong, Buzz Aldrin or any other man, 'and I know that, after going to hell and back within the confines of a loveless marriage, the product of a class whose corruption and hypocrisy have set in stone the institution of sexual infidelity, I shall one day find true happiness with a millionaire Arab playboy before meeting a tragic and untimely end'. Yup, it was all there in her eyes. But the British establishment – deafened by centuries of cotton wool placed oh-so-delicately in their ears by row upon row of liveried servants – refused to listen. Chinless wonders have no ears.

Charles committed the grossest act of sexual betrayal whilst poor Diana merely sought consolation from the stranglehold of her marriage in the arms of another human being. A maiden betrayed, plucky Diana candidly confessed her deep love for another person to millions of her devoted subjects. In the vicious manner of the English upper classes, cocksure Charles cruelly and coldly broadcast his adultery for everyone to hear. But the candle in the wind was about to bite back – and how.

So who was this Royal bloke – this man in trousers, this product of an outdated upper class, this twitchy faced defender of the sexual and hierarchical status quo – this nerd who Diana sat alongside in the Royal Carriage that cold, drizzly November afternoon as the reluctant horses, neighing and whinnying as if to say, 'Leave him, love', pulled the two of them back along the Kings Road after their wedding in St Paul's Abbey?

Charles was the product of a supremely dysfunctional family. One of his forebears – Henry – had divorced two of his wives and beheaded two more. Another – Elizabeth I – had placed those she disagreed with on piles of logs, bolstered them up with Zip firelighters embossed with the Royal logo and set fire to them. And yet another – Alfred – had, in a typically male frenzy of callous arson, burnt a senior citizen's cakes.

Charles's father, Philip, was a 'man's man', frightening,

sporty, given to arm-wrestling his wife before sitting down to a bedroom barbecue. Chastity was a stranger to him – but he knew Melanie, Fidelity and Trixie all too well. A simple browse through the Court Circular of the period reveals the range and variety of the married women Philip 'entertained' at his Central London love-nest, Buckingham Castle: in just one week in 1970, his so-called 'guests' included Mrs Brezhnev, Margaret Trudeau, Mary Wilson, Princess Grace of Monaco and Mrs Richard Nixon. Small wonder that his eldest son, socialised into this macho environment of misogyny, mayhem, malevolence, microbiology, and (COPY-EDITOR INSERT SOMETHING ELSE BEGINNING WITH M) was set to become the living embodiment of toffee-nosed sexism.

Charles, according to authoritative Royal biographer Kitty Kelley, was educated at Eton Academy, where he was forced to wear the traditional school uniform, designed for Queen Victoria, of long crinoline dress, high-heeled shoes and black silk brassière. Here, reveals Kelley, Charles first learnt to shoot baby seals at close range and, every morning before breakfast, to prove his manhood by placing his right arm inside the stomach of a dead sheep and supping on its entrails.

At Cambridge, he refused to follow the pursuits of the ordinary student. Not for Prince Snooty the 'Make Love Not War' T-shirt, the sit-in, the Che Guevara poster, the puking in the gutter after eight pints of Wadworth's Triple X, the mind-blowing spliff in the shared sleeping-bag while Pink Floyd's latest concept album blasted from the speakers: no, His Royal Snootiness preferred to indulge in the elite pastimes of his class, dressing up to murder household pets in the name of sport.

And what, then, of Diana? According to Kitty Kelley, author of authoritative biographies like *Bob Hope: Comedian and Serial-Killer* and *The Queen Mother: Slut*, the Prince's advisers chose her from a catalogue, and the Prince spoke to her only once before their marriage, turning to her at dinner one night and asking her to pass him the mashed potato. According to Bert Bung, for many years one of the most expert Royal-watchers on the *Daily Star*, two years after their marriage the Prince could not even remember her name, referring to her in official speeches as 'Princess Deirdre' or even 'Princess Darren'.

It was only after five long years of marriage that Charles first noticed the Princess of Wales was a woman. One evening, she wore an off-the-shoulder crinoline number, a ravishing dress that announced that here was no shrinking violet but a full-bosomed, broad-shouldered, wholly sexualised woman in the manner of Marilyn Monroe. Looking at herself in the mirror, Diana almost certainly thought, in her own words, 'Hey! This is me! I am woman! I am empowered by my burgeoning sexuality to challenge my containment in a patriarchal structure dominated by the class-based shibboleths of a past age. And yes, in the words of the legendary Gloria Gaynor – *"I will survive!"*'

Though I never 'knew' Diana in any tediously literal sense of the word, I did indeed *know* her in the far deeper sense of never having met her at all. *Her* in all her Herness, her HRHness, her HGVness, her HBpencilness. Diana, the working-class girl who took on the British aristocracy. Diana, the nursery-school teacher who rose to become the Oxford Professor of Modern Philosophy. No, Diana, we writers shall never, ever forget you, not for as long as sales permit.

X is for Xmas Blues

the secret meaning of christmas presents

We all have our faults. Mine? I'm not afraid to admit it: I have far too much creative energy. That, coupled with a craving for intellectual and artistic fulfilment – and a real flair for putting my millions of innovative ideas into action.

If you could listen to the inside of my head, it would sound something like this: 'Zap!' 'Whizz!' 'Eureka'. Of course, I'm simplifying. But listen harder and you would also hear a rich variety of warmer, gentler, more thoughtful and reflective noises: 'Purrrrr!' and 'Hmmmmm!' among them. Put it this way: I wear a lot of different hats. As a children's authoress, political adviser and senior *Guardian* columnist, I wear what I call my 'Zap' hat, I fizz with the interplay of ideas. But as a professional counsellor and relationships expert, with many television and radio appearances to my credit, I wear a different hat – a hat called 'Purrrr!', a hat called contemplation.

And I'd like to don this gentler, more analytic hat for this essay. The Secret Meaning of Christmas Presents dissects the motives behind different gifts your partner may be planning to give you – and offers a vital warning to women of all ages. Fuller details can be found in my recent publication *Coping With Christmas*, the latest in my 'Coping With . . .' series.

167

Other titles available in the series include *Coping With New Clothes, Coping With Old Friends* and *Coping With Your Days Off.*

The Household Item

Beware: he has stopped seeing you as a person and has started to see you only in terms of a housekeeper. If he gives you a steam-iron, a Hoover or 'something for the kitchen', you should run a mile. This guy is much more interested in his own judgement of what you need than in listening to your inner desires. Make a New Year's resolution: take control of your own life.

The Useless Item

Beware: if he gives you something entirely without practical value – a game, a toy, an expensive piece of jewellery – this means that he cannot come to terms with the fact that a woman is more than just a 'bit of fluff'. He is the boy who has never grown up. Inform him that you are a thinking person, and that – sorry, guys – you have absolutely no wish to act as a mother substitute. I once had a boyfriend who gave me a diamond ring. Two weeks later, we split up – and I never saw him again.

Sexy Underwear

You need to consider his opinion of you. Ask yourself if you really want to pander to his needs and fantasies. Beware – he may secretly be asking for physical attention. Take him to one side and tell him, gently but firmly, a) to keep his hands to himself and b) that you have decided to leave him for someone who gives you more space.

Designer Clothing

Such a gift signifies that your partner harbours deep-seated insecurities, particularly concerning women. He craves sub-liminal association with somebody else's upmarket image and feels that, by clothing you appropriately, he can turn you into just another expensive commodity for him to buy

168

and sell. I once went out with a guy who gave me a dress from Katharine Hamnett. Two weeks later, I left him.

Cosy Clothing
If he buys you the kind of 'sensible' underwear or sexless chainstore clothing your mother might wear – beware. Now is the time to take control of your life. He undoubtedly sees you as a mother substitute, and not as the full-blooded young woman you really are. He would prefer to ignore your sexual needs for an evening in front of the sport on television with a can of lager and a family packet of cheese and onion.

The Book or Record
The guy's a control freak, motivated by a compulsive need to direct all your thoughts towards the cultural, philosophical and political beliefs that he considers 'important'. But who the hell is he to judge? What has his boringly masculine view of the world to do with you? And if he likes the book or piece of music so much, why doesn't he get it for himself rather than off-loading it on you?

Confront him, and demand an explanation for his cultural imperialism. And ask yourself the simple question: is this really a relationship that was made to last?

A Holiday Abroad, A Meal Out, An Evening at the Theatre
Hold on a sec. Ask yourself how a man who could give you one or all of these can care about all that really matters, i.e. your company. Can't he appreciate you for who you really are, rather than constantly seeking the distraction of a meal out, a play or a trip abroad? And whatever you do, don't forget that many holidays and evenings out end in furious arguments, resulting in trial separation or even divorce. I once had a boyfriend who gave me a holiday in Mauritius. Two weeks later, we split up. And you know what? I never saw him again. Happy Christmas – if there is such a thing.

Y is for Yearning

what i really really want

I'll tell you what I want, what I really really want! Already, you, the reader, are utterly hooked, and don't pretend you're not because basically you're not fooling anyone.

As an award-winning journalist, even when I've been expressing far-ranging, nakedly personal and hugely complex views on the most serious issues, I've always made a point of getting in tune with the zeitgeist (love that word) of popular culture. Back in April 1975, commenting on the fall of Cambodia, I began my profoundly moving piece by declaring 'Mama mia, here we go again!' – because by that time not only were the Khmer Rouge riding into Phnom Penh but the truly formidable Abba were riding high in the charts with their unforgettable number 'Mama Mia'.

It caught the reader's attention, and that's what serious journalism is all about. Believe me, if I hadn't had the guts to tune into the zeitgeist at that time, hundreds of Abba fans would still have only the haziest idea about the whys and wherefores of the Cambodia situation, though I now forget exactly what they were. I used the same skill to incredible effect when Culture Club were zapping Britain to its knees in the early 1980s. I based my defiant and widely praised 5,000-word essay for the *New Statesman* condemning the post-imperial British invasion of the Falkland Islands on one of Boy George's most plangent lyrics. 'Do you really want to hurt me, Mrs Thatcher?' I asked at one point. 'Do you really want to make me cry?' As heartfelt outcries go, this was one that really did change hearts and minds.

I'll tell you what I want, what I really really want! See! I've done it again! Just as you were drifting off, I pulled you right back into the centre of an increasingly serious essay with a rendition from one of the most famous lyrics by the truly sensational Spice Girls. I've used that trick with this particular lyric two dozen – that's 24 – times so far and it always works a dream.

For instance, when I wanted to bolster up a hard-hitting article in the money pages on the continuing effect of Black Wednesday on Britain's economic future, I argued that, and I quote, 'firmer fiscal policy coupled with the possibility of long-term integration on an equal playing field must be what Britain wants, what Britain wants, what Britain really really wants, what Britain wants, what Britain wants what Britain really really wants in the distant and not-so distant economic and political future, when the greater obstacles to full monetary union are finally laid to rest.'

In this way, what might otherwise have been seen as a dry and arid intellectual debate on economic policy was turned into something much more vibrant and *now*. This meant it reached and touched the hearts of many millions of people – including those in the Treasury. When the economic history of Britain in the 1990s comes to be written, the influence of the Spice Girls will be seen as pivotal.

And let's never forget that the Spice Girls amount to one helluva lot more than just one catchy lyric. They are the spirit of 1997, and no serious commentator can afford to ignore them. That's why it's an open secret that all senior commentators on the *Guardian* have been issued with full lyric sheets of their latest hit single 'Mama', which is the personal favourite of my good mates and fellow commentators Hugo Young, Paul Foot and Peter Preston.

On the most superficial level, it is about the mothers of the Spice Girls ('Mama I love you, Mama I care/Mama I love you, Mama my friend/Mama I love you'), but this yearning for the mother-object is approachable on a great many deeper, more universal levels. That's why I have begun a lengthy essay on the future of EMU for the *Economist* with the searing opening, 'EMU I love you, EMU I care, EMU I love you, EMU my friend, EMU I love you: this is a statement to which many on the Left and Right would strongly object.'

At the same time, I cleverly employed a skilful variation on these lyrics in another piece I wrote for *Prospect* magazine on the future of democracy in Albania. Just as the article seemed in danger of becoming entrenched in the somewhat less-than-exciting muddy waters of history and analysis, I used my ingenuity to pep it up with a subliminal quote from the SGs. It's pretty subtle, but those in the final year of Media Studies courses may be able to spot it. 'Enver Hoxha,' I write, 'exerted an iron grip over the economy of Albania, and his influence continues to motivate many of those who might otherwise be tempted to say "Democracy I love you, democracy I care, democracy I love you, democracy my friend".'

And that's the way you get to be a leading commentator with your finger on the pulse of current events. Think Spice. 'Nuff said!

Z is for Zeitgeist Zeal

1997: the year of lots of different things happening at roughly the same time

It's a time not just for looking forward, but for looking back. As any driver will tell you, the best way to reach your destination is by never taking your eyes off the wing mirror. Basically, what we are is not just what we will be but also what we were, and we are what we might have been before we became what we would be once we had stopped being what we had been before we became what we were. It's as simple as that. 1997. 365 days. 52 weeks. 12 months. And literally hundreds of hours, minutes and seconds. A year like any other. But what a year!

It was the year Mike Tyson bit off his opponent's ear and the planet Hale Bopp astounded us with its sheer verve. Seminally, it was the year of the Teletubbies and David Helfgott, of Zoe Ball and Hong Kong. Yet what are we, the award-winning commentators, to make of these seemingly disparate events? Regarding the Mike Tyson story, on one level there is obviously a world-wide mood, a zeitgeist, if you will, of more and more people finding it morally defensible to bite off and chew minor parts of other people's bodies. Viewed from a certain angle, the planet Hale Bopp looked very much like the bottom section of a human ear: yet – eerily – the Teletubbies have no ears to speak of. Year ...

ear . . . no ear . . . eerie. Through the mist and fog of 365 days, a pattern fast emerges, a pattern as intricate yet vital, as ill-shapen yet emblematic as an ear.

It was the year of movement. There were one helluva lot of people on the move in 1997. Martin Amis announced he was moving to America. Swampy moved in and out of tunnels. William Hague went to India for his honeymoon. Humphrey the Cat, bless him, moved out of Number 10. The Spice Girls completed their seminal world tour. Woody Allen and Soon-Yi travelled all the way to Italy to get married in Venice. The planet Hale-Bopp moved across our skies to astound us with its sheer verve. And, as chronicled in my series of hilariously offbeat articles in the *Observer*, I myself made the move from Kentish Town to Islington – taking my three irascible moggies with me!

Ears; movement; Zoe Ball; Martin Amis; Hale-Bopp; Hong Kong; the Tamagotchi; me. Looking back, it seems that everything was leading inexorably to the death of Diana, Princess of Wales. Like Zoe Ball, she was a thoroughly modern woman who touched all our hearts. Like Tamagotchis, she seemed at times to be operated by forces beyond her control. Like Hong Kong, as a child she was handed from one parent to the other. Like Martin Amis, she helped define a generation. And like Hale-Bopp, she was a star, a planet, a veritable constellation, never more bountifully herself than when illuminating up the night sky with her radiance.

Like the unnerving, brilliant and deeply disturbing 'Sensation' exhibition at the Royal Academy, the collapse of the tiger economies, the unstoppable spread of BSE and the damning report on the Royal Opera House, the death of Diana, Princess of Wales on the last day of August was a shocking reminder of quite how shocking some reminders can be. Even through our tears we were surprised by what we saw; we didn't realise how much we had changed. We were not the country we thought we were, or the country they wanted us to be: with all the deft fingerwork of one who excelled at needlework at her secondary school, Diana had unbuttoned our emotions.

I wept; you wept; he or she wept; we wept; you plural wept; they wept: we all wept. We wept not only for Diana, Princess of Wales, but for ourselves. Who would now visit us in hospital? Who would wipe away those tears? Who would argue our cause with the powerful? Who would now get on the exercise bike on our behalf and keep us in trim? Who would accompany us in a bewitching new swimsuit to our sun-soaked Mediterranean hideaways? Who would tell the outmoded Royal Family just what we thought of them and their hoity-toity ways?

Through our tears, we recognised a new Britain, a Britain we could live in, a seminal Britain surrounded by sea yet with a fair bit of dry land too, a Britain with roads, buildings, wide open spaces and a variety of outlets to satisfy the tastes of even the most discerning shopper. This was our Britain, not theirs: it was a Britain for the Spice Girls and Girl Power, for the heroic Swampy and the smashing Clare Short, for Martin Bell and Zoe Ball, for Tony Banks and the Teletubbies, for Dolly the Sheep and David Helfgott, for Cherie and Tony, for the Millennium Dome and some truly powerful and inventive regional theatre. Truly, 1997 was the year in which the tragic death of Diana lit a Candle in the Wind, and, believe me, this is one candle that will never go out when the sunset appears through the snow above the clouds through the howling rain at the rainbow's end. In a nutshell, 1997 was a year – and a year we shall truly never see again.

Z is also for Zip

who played bass on the third track, second side of ummagumma?

It's a little-known fact that the Prime Minister has the most encyclopaedic knowledge of rock music this side of the great John Peel. Who played bass on the third track, second side of *Ummagumma*? In what month of which year did *Bat out of Hell* first reach number 1 in the UK charts? Leonard Cohen has written five songs with women's christian names in their titles – can you name four? These are just some of the questions that Tony Blair got a hundred per cent right in the Great New Labour Rock'n'Roll Trivia Quiz we staged on Concorde on the flight over to Washington.

There was a spirit of exhilaration on the plane as Peter Mandelson handed out the rock'n'roll trivia quiz sheets to the assembled company. And what a company it was! Tony and Alistair had gathered together the pick of the British rock establishment to match the best that Washington could offer. 'Greetings, pop-pickers! All right? Stay bright! Not arf!' It was the distinctive voice of Alan 'Fluff' Freeman over the captain's telecom, welcoming us aboard – and giving us our first real taste of Cool Britannia, export-style. Fluff had agreed to introduce the Prime Minister for his grand entrance at the White House dinner ('Greetings, pop-pickers Stateside! And here's the mellow, mellow sound of our very own Prime Minister. All right? Stay bright! Not arf!'), and now he was setting us at ease for the journey of a lifetime.

It was a time of high spirits. 'You forgot your portfolio, mate!' said Alastair Campbell to Peter Mandelson as he returned to his seat.

'I don't *have* a portfolio – and you know it!' snapped back Peter, testily. Sensing an air of friction, Tony stepped in. 'Anyone remember who played violin on "All Around My Hat"?'

' "All Around My Hat"? Wasn't that Pentangle?' chipped in Alastair.

'Du-urr! It's Steeleye Span! What a total thicko! Shows how much *you know*!' said Peter.

'Is right! Stay bright!' exclaimed Fluff. 'Not arf!'

Just then, our special in-flight rock'n'roll artiste came on to perform his first set. It seems years since I last saw Rick Wakeman, but he was on truly rockin' form, performing a masterly rendition of *The Six Wives of Henry VIII*, his three keyboards and synthesiser taking up most of the lounge area, the second keyboard stretching right into the cockpit: at one point he hit a wrong key and the airplane automatically re-routed for Buenos Aires.

But it was soon back on course. 'Great stuff, Rick!' said Tony, bringing out his old Fender and asking Wakey to teach him the opening chords to 'Catherine Parr' so as to knock 'em all sideways at the White House ball.

And so to Washington. I'm not being elitist or anything, but I can truly say that the cream of British equality minded society was out in force. Not just Tina and Harry (incidentally, Tina was thrilled because she'd just bought a brilliant short story for the *New Yorker* by Karla Faye Tucker, and the recent execution has given it the most brilliant publicity boost) but other great names like Sting and Ron Wood and Mike Robb from Chicory Tip.

It was, in its way, a celebration of New Labour's whole new outlook on outdated notions like the 'Establishment' and 'privileged elites'. Tony and Bill are members of the rock'n'roll generation – and there's one helluva lot of elitist cobwebs they want to brush away. As you'd imagine, Tony and Bill and Cherie and Hillary were on the top table, with Elton and Sting on the second table, but I was just fifteen tables away, in a mainly media circle with our very own Richard Madeley and Judy Finnegan, David Montgomery, Vanessa Feltz, Sir David Frost, Fern Britton, Loyd Grossman, Rod Hull and Emu and the lead singer of Kajagoogoo. I kept an eye open for Alastair Campbell and the Minister without Portfolio, but they were literally rushed off their feet helping with the eats.

Needless to say, we were on tenterhooks over the promised jam-session. Would Tony and Bill boogie on down, kick out the jams and knock us sideways with a rousing duet for sax and lead guitar? First, Rick Wakeman played from a work-in-progress, his new symphony for banjo and tuba, *The Two Wives of Robin Cook*, then Sting sang unaccompanied through his moving, plangent twenty-seven minute 'Elegy for a Rainforest', during which dinner-guests were permitted to talk among themselves and make use of the conveniences. Finally – yes! – Tony and Cherie were persuaded up onstage by Bill and Hillary. Together, the four of them soared their way through a great rendition of 'You Sexy Thing' from the British hit movie *The Full Monty*, accompanied by Tina Brown on harp and Harry Evans on spoons. A truly magical, left-of-centre evening – and a scorching signpost for the years ahead.

Supplement
With Tony to Victory: My New Labour Diary

1 January 1996

After seventeen long, cold years of Tory rule, the New Year has started with a shot in the arm. I met the great Janet Street-Porter when we appeared together on Germaine Greer's mould-breaking all-woman New Year chat-show on the Beeb.

I don't suppose anyone will ever forget this, the third in the series, least of all me. Halfway through a sentence, I broke down and just sobbed and sobbed and sobbed and sobbed. The subject under discussion was the place of women in our society, and I had just been telling Janet and the others how I know that our Shadow Home Secretary, Jack Straw, is a guy who really understands women, who really knows what concerns us. 'He may seem just like any other happy-go-lucky kinda guy,' I said, 'but he's caring and he's gentle and when he puts those great big Jacky arms around you, he makes you think you're the only girl in the – the – the . . . I'm sorry, oh my god, I can't go on.'

It was Janet who came to my rescue. 'Anyone here been to the new Damien Hirst show at the Serpentine?' she said, changing the subject as I took ten deep breaths. ''Cos it's really TATB, by which I mean Truly Amazing Totally Brill. Now there's a guy who really *does* understand what women are going through in the second half of the 20th century. I tell you, he's right up there with Kurt Cobain.'

After the show was over, Janet asked me to go with her to the Hirst show tomorrow. 'It's TMBX,' she said, 'by which I mean Truly Mind Blowing.'

'But what about the "X",' I said.

'I just put that in for effect,' she replied.

2 January 1996

On arrival at the Serpentine, I found my mind well and truly blown. Damien creates haunting images you just can't forget, in much the same way as the original art work for the cover of *Close to the Edge* by Yes that hangs on my bedroom wall. Hirst's 'What'll We Do Once it's Over?' is an upturned turtle, its legs still wriggling. 'Maybe Get a Bite to Eat' is a ping-pong ball resting in the mouth of a goldfish, and 'Or Just Go Straight Home and Watch TV if You'd Rather' is a sofa cut in two, making a couple of very reasonably sized armchairs with one arm each. As we say goodbye, Janet asks me for dinner on Thursday. She says there's someone she'd like me to meet.

5 January 1996

To dinner with Janet. Her special guest? Damien Hirst! Janet was serving Damien raw ox-head with tongue as a tribute. 'Will you carve?' she asked, and Damien got out his chain-saw, but I just had the fur, being a fully paid-up vegetarian.

8 January 1996

Great to see Janet S-P's back where she belongs, in her very own column at the bottom of page 7 of the *Observer* every second week. Today, she wrote a brilliantly articulated piece arguing that Damien was the front-runner for the Turner Prize. 'Just forget the ceremony and give the guy his reward,' she said. 'He brings people into the gallery who'd never go otherwise . . .'

A thought suddenly struck me. Why the hell can't we in New Labour utilise Damien's extraordinary talents? Remember how my own brainchild, Red Wedge, helped carry us all the way through to second place in '92? Well, Damien could help us repeat the same trick in '97!

12 January 1996

I raise the Hirst project at our bi-weekly round-table New Labour media discussion group. Jack Straw was there, and so was John Prescott, whose jacket sleeve was absolutely drenched on account of his cold. Jack gave a preliminary briefing. He wanted to make it clear that the Old Labour words 'the poor' should be changed in all election material to 'the low achievers in our society'. Then he called for any bright ideas for a New Labour logo to replace the hugely successful Red Rose. I seized the opportunity and placed a large plastic bag in the middle of the table.

I unwrapped the package and put a dead rabbit sawn in half on the table. Some of the blood started seeping its way towards Jack's interim report on underage low achievers in the East Midlands. 'It's a Damien Hirst,' I said, my voice swelling with pride. 'The two sides of the dead rabbit symbolise the two sides of Labour – new and old – coming together in a shared spirit of optimism. And what's more Damien's designed rabbit neck-ties – two ears apiece – to be worn by all the Shadow Cabinet in the lead-up to the election. In my opinion, the bisected rabbit will make all the right noises to the electorate. Any questions?' I could tell by their utter silence that Jack and John were literally over the moon. Wear your dead rabbit with pride!

I was in full flow. 'I want to see a fairer Britain,' I said, 'a Britain at ease with itself. A Britain where a poor person can walk down the street without blocking the way of the better off. A Body Shop Britain, where courageous people like Anita Roddick are allowed to sell their excellent skin products with the minimum of hassle from the dinosaurs of the union movement. And I want to see a modern, vibrant Labour Party, a party in tune with the aspirations of the achievers in our society, a party willing to reverse its tired old dogma about taking from the rich and giving to the poor, a party ready to create a new, leaner Britain, where initiative, risk-taking and wealth-creation are given their just rewards!'

Philip Gould had taken me to lunch at Le Gavroche to discuss how to make New Labour a party not only for the better off, but a party that's also prepared to listen from time to time to the endless complaints of the less well off.

'I like to imagine a time, Bel,' I remember him saying, 'when this restaurant will be literally packed out with people on the minimum wage.'

'My god, I agree with that vision, Phil,' I said, looking around me for the wine waiter, 'it's very clearly understaffed at the moment.'

Phil then did me the greatest honour of my life when he invited me to join Tony's Advisory Team, as Peter Mandelson's eyes and ears. 'Peter has to spend a lot of his time on more important things,' explained Phil. 'So he wants you to keep him in touch with what the ordinary people in the street are thinking.'

I got back to my car flushed with the challenge ahead. As the driver eased his way past Marble Arch, I was already sifting through my address book for ordinary people.

'Barbara – it's Bel,' I yelled down the mobile to the lovely Barbara Follett. 'Phil Gould's asked me to ask you what you're thinking.'

Barbara told me she was thinking autumnal hues, she

was thinking horse-chestnuts and falling leaves, she was thinking oranges and browns and deep, deep reds. I jotted it all down. Something tells me Phil will be over the moon.

24 January 1996

My very first appearance as a member of Tony's Advisory Team. Phil Gould was president and he explained our jobs. Phil is in charge of supplementing the message, Peter is in charge of implementing the message, Jonathan is in charge of coordinating the message, Alastair is in charge of disseminating the message and I'm in charge of asking around to see if anyone has managed to find the message yet.

We'll make a great team. No matter what the snipers say, the Labour Party's major objective is now clearly defined: it is to find our major objective. By the time that meeting had ended, we had laid out the foundation for the command structure for the implementation of the strategy for the foundation for a command structure for a Labour victory, a coherent strategy policy to see us through the next two elections:

4.1 Autumnal hues. BL to advise TB on radical rethink employing oranges and browns and deep, deep reds. Would TB be more electable with moustache?

4.2 Focus on moustache. CA (Clem Attlee) led Old Labour to great victory in 1945 wearing moustache. JC (James Callaghan), MF (Michael Foot) and NK (Neil Kinnock) rejected all moustache options, lost elections.

4.3 Moustache selection and cultivation. BL to consult JS-P (Janet Street-Porter) on type of moustache to appeal to first-time voter. PM to oversee presentation: design, growth, trimming, etc.

4.4 Moustache schedule. Deadline for TB moustache: autumn 1995 at Labour conference. Choice of slogan by PG. Strong possibility: 'New Labour, New Whiskers'.

5.1 Need to find Big Message. PG and PM to organise major ground search.

5.2 Upon finding Big Message, differences between Tory Big Message and New Labour Message to be maximised in clear policy statements.

5.3 Establish clear differences in approach in lead-up to election: TB has new moustache to offer electorate; JM (John Major) has no new moustache. Victory assured.

19 February 1996

Another day, another high-powered set lunch for like-minded radicals in a discreet but far from uninteresting new restaurant. There comes a time in everyone's life when you've simply got to sit down and be counted. 'Change is gonna come,' sang the late, great Marvin Gaye. The format is simple. First, you change for lunch. And then you lunch for change. It's worth it, you know, even if you don't get much change out of £30 a head, excluding service. Intended result? A complete overhaul of our outdated hierarchical structures, and the prospect of a truly modern, democratic republic by the year 2000.

It's by now an open secret that I was a founder-member of what is now acknowledged as one of the greatest of our post-war radical lunch groups, the Campden Hill Square Set. Held in Ms Lady Antonia Fraser's home, not much more than a mile or so from Acton and only four miles in a cab from Brixton, it consisted of people like John Mortimer and Melvyn Bragg – people very, very peckish for change.

Those were the days. We would arrive at 12.30 for 1.00 in smart-but-casual wear. So as to cut down on the cost of clothes, our treasurer, David Hare, had arranged discounts at Nicole Fahri outlets for all members, on production of a current membership card. Our coats would be taken by Ms Lady Antonia Fraser's co-workers, Dolores and Felipe, who would then retire to the kitchen to continue their discussions on workers' rights.

At 1.00 sharp, the debate would start. John Mortimer would propose Leoni's Quo Vadis. Too far, too soon, David would counter: we wouldn't arrive at our destination until it was too late, and the chips were already down. The debate would then be thrown open to the floor. Antonia would suggest Le Caprice, arguing that it represented an entirely open society at a price worth paying. She would then be shouted down by Harold, who favoured the strong, more directly peasant-like flavours issuing from the River Café. Passions would now be at their height. Harold would walk out, saying that choosing Quo Vadis would be just like bombing Hanoi all over again, only more expensive. Contrary to what its critics would have us believe, the Campden Hill Square Set achieved its aim of becoming the *forum* for civilised debate until it broke up in disarray amidst accusation and counter-accusation just six months later.

Weeks later, in the upstairs' room of The Ivy, over canapés of twiglets shaped as parliamentary portcullises, Charter 88 was formed. The number – 88 – honoured the two original signatories, Clare Rayner and Miriam Margolyes, and the title paid tribute to the last great Democratic president of the US, Jimmy Charter.

And today I schlepp along to the Common Sense Club, a gang of republicans who believe passionately that the people should wrest democratic power from the elite. We meet regularly in Charlotte Street's exclusive L'Etoile, always in a private room so that ordinary diners won't overhear our democratic discussions – or worse, be tempted to join in.

Basically, we are all fiercely anti-monarchist, none more so than that great republican polemicist Tony Holden, author of *Charles: Prince of Men* (1972), *Charles and Diana: a Marriage Made in Heaven* (1981), *Charles and Diana: a Crowning Love* (1989), *God Bless You, Ma'am: a Celebration of Queen Elizabeth, the Queen Mother* (1991), *Prince Edward: TV Producer of Genius* (1994) and, most recently, *The Monarchy: a Serious Reappraisal* (1996), in which he argues that an absurdly rosy, cosy view of the Royal Family has been foisted on the people by unscrupulous journalists, interested more in profit than in truth.

Tony chaired the meeting. The debate started as we were taking our seats. 'These chairs are a bit uncomfortable, aren't they? Can I put it to the membership of the Common Sense Club to vote for a change of chairs?' demanded Professor Stephen Haseler. On a point of information, Michael Mansfield then kindly pointed out that the chairs were still stacked on each other top-to-bottom: the Professor had been attempting to sit on the upturned legs. But before long the Common Sense Club got into its stride. 'A grown-up, educated people simply doesn't need to defer to so-called superiors with fancy titles!' I announced, to a round of applause from some of the biggest names in left-wing politics.

Over pudding Tony Benn had an announcement to make. 'You may remember,' he said, 'at our last meeting we sanctioned a letter to Her Majesty explaining our brave stand against the Monarchy. I'm now delighted to say we have received a handwritten reply from Buckingham Palace thanking us on behalf of the Queen, no less, for our kind letter, confirming she read it with the very greatest of interest and wishing us all the very best of luck with our project.' He then passed the letter around for us all to look at. A buzz of radical pride swept through the company. Take it from me, there's nothing like knowing your efforts are appreciated by the people who really matter.

Good Friday, 5 April 1996

Down to Easter in the country with truly smashing friends, since you asked (not!). No, but seriously, I have schlepped down to spend a very happy Easter with Barbara and Ken Follett in their modest, in-keeping house right in the heart of the beautiful, warm-hearted constituency with so much real character which Barbara is set to win with a large majority come the General Election. I think it begins with an 'S' or just possibly a 'P', but Barbara remains convinced it's a 'T'. She says she'll know for certain when the headed notepaper arrives, bless her.

Easter Saturday, 6 April 1996

It'll be really nice when they've expanded it down to the end of the street after the election. Barbara and Ken are doing great things with the house. And the proposed staff block just across the street will be fabulously handy, decorated with a vivid, get-up-and-go colour of the staff's own choice – democratically chosen by secret ballot from a short list of attractive light pinks drawn up by Barbara herself.

Fellow snug Easter bunnies in the Follett nest are the much-maligned Peter Mandelson (give him a break, guys), my old chum Jack Straw plus ace slide guitar, and the lovely Harriet Harman. This morning, we put on our oldest clothes just to mosey around the constituency, getting to know the lovely warm people of S–. Come lunchtime, we bought some smashing ready-cooked fish and chips from a real live fish-and-chip shop in the middle of the market, shoving on great wads of vinegar and salt and ketchup. We managed to eat quite a few mouthfuls in front of appreciative constituents before schlepping back to Barbara's for a fabulous lunch of Olive, Bacon and Endive Salad followed by Peasant Chicken with Sun-Dried Tomatoes from Ruthie Rogers' brilliant *River Café Cook Book*.

The evening was really great, with Jack strumming along to some old King Crimson faves and Harriet singing 'I'd Like to Teach the World to Sing (in Perfect Harmony)' in memory of her days in the New Seekers. Pete had never heard the song before – he was heavily into the King's Singers at the time – but he was sure Tony would think it just right for the New Labour theme tune at the election. 'Tony in the middle, singing his heart out, and Cookie and Prescott on either side in their New Labour flared jump-suits, clicking their fingers and miming along as though in perfect harmony. Fan-tastic!'

Later, talk came round to Tony, as it always does. 'I really like the guy,' said Jack.

'Yeah, me too,' enthused Barbara.

'I've always found him a really likeable kinda bloke,' ventured Ken.

'Yeah,' said Peter, 'thoroughly likeable. And I think he'll make a smashing Prime Minister.'

'A great Prime Minister,' said Harriet.

'Our greatest Prime Minister since the war,' said Jack.

'This century,' chipped in Barbara.

'Ever,' I added. And at that point I sensed everyone knew I had won the discussion. As I went to sleep, I wondered if Tony knew just how loyal we all were, and whether he realised that I, Bel Littlejohn, was the most loyal of them all.

Easter Sunday, 7 April 1996

Easter Sunday, and we all leapt on the Sunday rags. Frankly, the first thing I always read is the likes of Wallace Arnold to see what the other side is thinking, then I turn to the Peregrine Worsthorne column in *The Sunday Torygraph*, though they say he's one of those made-up characters. It was while I was looking for this column in the *Torygraph* that I noticed the headline – 'Why I am a Christian, by Tony Blair'.

I yelped with delight. The others came rushing to my side and read it over my shoulders, the smell of Jack's Brut for Men wafting seductively into my face. 'I'm off to church,' Peter Mandelson announced suddenly. 'Anyone know whether the very best seats are still available?'

'I always go to church at Easter,' said Harriet.

'Me too!' added Jack. 'And even at Christmas, if there's a church open!'

'I go at New Year and Bank Holidays, plus Guy Fawkes' Day, weather permitting,' said Ken.

'I'm training to be a deacon in Tony's regular church in Islington,' I informed them. Silence ensued, and they all pursed their lips, busily thinking Christian thoughts.

We all read the piece right to the end. It was Peter who broke the silence. 'As always, Tony's so right,' he said. 'I mean, it wasn't easy for Pontius Pilate or Judas Iscariot, was it? Christianity was going through a period of transition. Tough decisions were required for the greater goal of long-term economic and social stability. Pontius was determined not to alienate the homeowners, and Judas strongly believed in promoting greater understanding among all those Christians with a modest amount of capital to invest in the future prosperity of their country.'

'Nuff said. In New Labour, we're all very, very Christian these days, and we don't care who knows it, just as long as Tony does. And Peter Mandelson's brave new book *The Pontius Revolution: Keep Your Hands Clean with New Labour* should be in the shops by next Easter. Praise the Lord!

29 April 1996

Love 'em to pieces. Oasis, I mean. Five lads – Noel Gallagher, Liam Gallagher and three others, all with their own different names – who, put together, sure make me wanna boogie. Managed to catch their gig today at the Manchester City stadium, and what a great gig it's turned out to be, with all of us singing our hearts out with the majestic Liam as he chanted that legendary Oasis chorus, with its sublimated references to Shakespeare, John Donne and Virginia Woolf, 'No, Sally can't weigh/She knows it's too lay/She's a dad di di da-di-dy-y.'

Magic. And what made the gig so powerfully moving was that it was the lads saying a big 'thank you' to their fans in lovely, lovely Manchester, the city that nurtured their geniuses and gave them the courage to carry on when times were hard. And as a way of thanking the greatest fans in the world, Liam and Noel took no more than £17.50 a head from each of them, just to cover their hotel and travelling expenses, etc. In return they sang their hearts out on a stage no more than a hundred yards away for well over an hour.

Charging less than £20 for most tickets, apart from those with a view of the stage, was their way of thanking the working-class youth of Manchester for making them into the millionaires they are today. Cheers, Manchester!

Youth culture. That's where the action is, and I'm proud to write for a newspaper that gives it the attention it deserves. Incidentally, the *Guardian* also springs from Manchester – snap! – and at the moment I'm gathering a group of *Guardian* writers to play a 'thank-you' stadium gig, with Bea Campbell, Pete Preston, Suzanne Moore and yours truly singing our guts out to some classy Hugo Young tracks such as 'Whither the SDP' (1967), a 'Future for the ERM' (1992), and – my all-time favourite – 'Setbacks in Store for Thatcher?' (1983). 'Nuff said.

30 April 1996

There's so much energy and sheer unabashed, unadulterated vitality in youth culture. The young have got so much to say, and it's high time we listened to 'em. Janet Street-Porter, for instance: I'm always interested in what she's got to say: Vivienne Westwood ditto; and I've also got one helluva lot of time for Jimmy Savile. They're all remarkable role-models for young people.

We in New Labour are desperate to channel some of this vitality to ram us home to victory at the next election. Obviously, to have Oasis on board will be a tremendous feather in our cap, sending out the message to young people like Janet and Vivienne that we really do care about the very real issues that affect the young people of today, such as 'wicked' clothes, continental lager and 'rap' music.

So today I was proud to return to another Oasis concert as Chair of a New Labour Youth Delegation to watch Liam and the guys from a special VIP room backstage, well away from all the noise. Obviously, the ever-youthful Jack Straw was on our list. Jack specially changed into his tie-dye T-shirt and orange crushed velvet loons with 12-inch flares for the occasion. Harriet Harman and the lovely Clare Short were also on board, though I had to have a quiet word in Clare's ear about joining in the choruses on some of the band's more controversial numbers. Finally, the much-maligned Peter Mandelson was with us, keen as ever to persuade the lads into dropping a plug for New Labour's plans for a Stakeholder Society into one of the show-stopping choruses. 'Oh, Stakeholder Society can't weigh/She says it's too lay/She's da di di da-di-dy-y' was Jack's provisional draft, but he told us he'd welcome amendments.

1 May 1996

Back for my third(!) rockin' good night with Oasis, again with the others in tow – 'cos tonight we had been promised a meeting with the guys themselves! And our dream came true: we were deeply privileged to be introduced to Noel, Liam and the three others just before they went on stage. Jack was the first to get a discussion going: 'Might I just have a quick word with you, lads, about the dreadful pest that's nibbling away at the root of our society – namely the Squeegee Merchants?' From where I was standing, I thought Liam looked fascinated and as always he expressed his enthusiasm in a forceful fashion. 'Fook of, four-eyes,' he said, tapping Jack affectionately on the nose with his fist.

'Love it!' said Jack as he picked himself up off the floor, his grin a little lop-sided as he dabbed his blood-soaked nose with the Quik-Wipes he always carries with him. Harriet then roared into bridge-building mode, asking Noel if they'd play one of her all-time favourites, 'Mull of Kintyre'. 'Incidentally, has anyone ever told you that you sound a bit like Wings?' she asked.

'You tryin' to wind me up or what? You could do with a right bottlin', you could,' replied Noel. As I helped Harriet up from the floor, I could think only one thing: so much youthful passion – and in one so young!

I just know Noel and Liam will be the ideal entertainers

for this year's £500-a-head New Labour fund-raising bash at the Dorchester. And I know they wouldn't mind us teaching them how to hold their knives and forks properly in an emergency session beforehand. Great lads. Great music. Take it away!

30 May 1996

I love a party with a happy atmosphere – particularly when it's a party for the Party(!). All true former socialists and believers in New Labour are busily preparing for the party of the year. Next Thursday, we're off to Barbara Follett's pad in north Battersea, just across the river from the park, for a lunch to celebrate the 47th birthday of the man who just happens to be her husband.

Barbara and Ken are often cruelly lampooned by the tabloid gutter press just for having stuck to their principles. They've been through a helluva lot in the last few years: upwards of four hundred thou, if I've got my sums right. But they've made their house in West Victoria not just a home, but a real *community*, keeping in touch with ordinary decent working people by employing them to oversee the simpler household chores such as shopping and cleaning, all the time lending a listening ear to what they really have to say about ordinary life.

'But what are the ordinary people in the street saying about my selection as Labour candidate for S–?' Barbara was asking Dolores, her personal assistant (laundry, floors, polishing), when I popped round today to help with the admin over a refreshing cup of camomile tea. 'Are they as thrilled as I am?'

'Yes, ma'am,' replied Dolores, concealing her delight behind a mischievous frown.

'Yes, *Barbara* – please. We're a *community*, don't forget.'

'Yes, Barbara.'

'And when you've finished the sprouts, could you have a go at the silver?'

Barbara's life is a hectic treadmill of delegation, supervision and inspection, yet somehow she still manages to find time to keep in touch with the grass roots. She's very proud of her little house in S–, bless her. It's nothing too grand, but she wants to show the electors of S– she really cares about local issues: the way young couples are being driven away from the area by wealthy out-of-towners buying up the available property as second homes, etc., etc. How I wish the knockers would stop accusing Barbara of hypocrisy without first checking their facts. S– is not, I repeat, *not*, her second home. After London and the south of France, it's her third, and, like a youngest child, it has a very warm, special place in her heart.

1 June 1996

Plans for Ken's birthday party are gathering pace. Contrary to tabloid tittle-tattle Tony and Cherie have accepted!

2 June 1996

Well, not accepted exactly, bless 'em – they both said they'd really love to be there but Tony, poor love, has agreed to take the kids swimming, and Cherie's dad might be staying, and the traffic can be terrible at that time of day. And, after all, Tony's busy preparing for government – give the guy a break!

4 June 1996

Well, Jack Straw was there, which was great. Ken and Barbara had insisted that 'smart/casual' was the order of the day – they're delightfully smart/casual through and through – and Jack wore his tank-top and velvet loons, 'cos the guy's young at heart. In fact, by way of 'breaking the ice' he reminded us that he's on course to be our very first Home Secretary with a complete framed set of all the Yes album-cover posters on his living-room walls – and that certainly can't be bad for democracy.

Who else was there? Obviously the Folletts couldn't accommodate every single person in S–, though God knows they'd dearly love to have done, because they've come to know and love S– so much that they can find their way there without even looking at a map. Instead they asked the Chair of the Constituency Association, which is really lovely of them, though not for the finger buffet following, as they would hate him or her to feel in any way awkward or out of her or his depth.

Everyone was there. Harriet (Harman) had promised to put her head round the door on her way back from lacrosse, and I'm pretty sure she did though I might have been in the kitchen at the time. And there was the cream of 'showbiz' too! That smashing comedian Ben Elton recorded a special birthday message for Ken, to be played in Ben's absence, and Barbara managed to press the lovely John Prescott into coat duty, bless him.

To be honest, the staff were almost as excited as the rest of us, agreeing a substantial reduction in overtime in return for the chance to mingle. And Chef baked an amazing multi-layered Ken Tribute cake, its base shaped like an electric guitar, because Ken, for all his extraordinary literary sophistication – he reckons he's in with a good chance for the Booker this year – is basically an old rocker at heart. The second layer was designed as a New Labour Gold Member-ship Card, with portraits in icing of the party's ten wealthiest contributors, symbolising Ken's passionate commitment to the advancement of the working class.

And the top layer! You got it. It was a portrait in sponge of Barbara, surrounded by a collage in icing sugar of the latest world sales figures for each of Ken's last ten bestsellers. Simple, but effective. Wicked party, brill people. As Barbara said to Dolores in the early hours when we were all totally out of it, 'We didn't want anything too showy – after all, we're very feet-on-the-ground sort of people. Oh, and if you could tackle that stain on the second landing . . .'

18 July 1996
Provence

It's funny, but whenever I set foot in La France, I feel as though in a curious way I've come home – though obviously I don't actually come home until the holiday has ended. Warm *croissants*, strong coffee, mixed salads, dry white wine, *pommes frites*, olive oil: yup, it's great to get back to good old Sainsbury's once it's all over.

For the past five years, I've holidayed with the Folletts in their luxury villa. But this summer Barbara is tied up in S–. She thinks it would send out the wrong vibes to the electorate if she were seen to be vacationing anywhere too obviously 'out of reach', so she and Ken have decided to spend a few days beneath the tropical sun-lamps in the S– Solarium and Swirl-Pool Centre. Barbara says she's looking forward to the experience very much. 'There's nothing like S– Solarium and Swirl-Pool Centre for closing your eyes and imagining you're somewhere really nice,' she says in full-colour leaflets delivered through the doors of over 15,000 key electoral households in the constituency.

So this year I've accepted an invitation to come here to Provence with Jack Straw and his smashing family. In our preliminary first-morning meeting to thrash out a draft amendment to the proposed holiday schedule, Jack promised to bring out his guitar one night and play a selection of his all-time fave raves. 'I'll be doing a rockin' good version of "Massachusetts" by The Squee Gees,' he announced.

'The Bee Gees,' I corrected him. 'Jack, you're becoming a workaholic.'

19 July 1996

Together with Michael Meacher, we start to work our way through the Peter, Paul and Mary song-book. These singalongs are something of a tradition on the Straw holidays: last year, Jack and his holiday guest Margaret

195

Beckett performed a military two-step version of 'Voulez-Vous Couchez Avec Moi (Ce Soir)', with Robin Cook accompanying them on bagpipes, bless 'em.

21 July 1996

Jack's a meticulous holiday-organiser, never leaving anything to chance. This makes it ultra luxurious for everyone else. For instance, each bottle of wine is clearly marked so there's no muddle-up about who's drunk what. Today, we went out to a local bistro, and Jack brought along his pocket calculator so when I pointed out that I hadn't ordered any salad, he extracted the proportion of the cost from my share of the bill. But I hope that doesn't make it all sound like so much hard work, 'cos it's nothing of the sort: morning roll-call isn't until a luxurious 9.30, and we all take turns with the clipboard.

26 July 1996

For me, holidays are all about books. When I go on holiday, I read and read and read and read, especially if there's half an hour before dinner. I love books for their smell, and the way they feel. I love books for their portability, and the sound of flick-flick-flick as you riffle through their pages. I love books for the way each page has a different number at the bottom, and each successive number is one higher than the last. I love books for their bindings, and for their spines. And quite often I manage to get right through to the end of one, pressure of time permitting. Personally, I always try to take books that give me a flavour of the country I'm in: *Paris Trout* in France, or *All Quiet on the Western Front* in Truro. So it's not surprising that all the literary editors have been on at me to give them my holiday reading lists: who can blame ordinary readers for wishing to follow the example of a celebrity book-lover rather than make some sort of faulty, ill-informed choice for themselves?

196

27 July 1996

My own much-thumbed deck-chair reads include the latest books by Will Hutton and Andrew Marr on how the hell we're gonna get out of the dire situation we find ourselves in, if and when that dire situation comes about, if it hasn't already. Personally, I can't wait to see how their books end. But for something a little more tender, a little more tearful, a little more sincere, I've been enjoying the latest Peter Mandelson. It's a lovely, warm-hearted book with, coincidentally, a hero called Peter and a vivid minor character called Tony, who helps him. Together, they save the world, or at least give it a jolly good polish – I'll be finishing it on the flight back, the perfect end to a perfect holiday.

3 August 1996

Truly wicked time at the first of our New Labour outings to the races in Berks. Contrary to what the anti-Murdoch tabloids might have us believe, the Berks racecourse in question – popularly known as Ascot – is not remotely 'grand'. Far from it. It's filled with lots of ordinary, decent people of the sort we are hoping to tempt into backing the New Labour horse to romp home at the next election. And sure enough, by the end of the day quite a few of them were wearing our specially designed red-on-white 'BERKS FOR NEW LABOUR' stickers on their top hats.

The lovely Robin Cook is himself a former jockey. He once rode in the Derby. Sadly, halfway through, his donkey grew restless and threw him off. Ever since, Robin has been an enthusiastic spectator. But he's an incorrigible workhorse too, even bringing his long-suffering secretary Miss Regan along to take notes whenever they can find somewhere suitably quiet, like a field of hay. In fact, his whole philosophy of New Labour has been formulated through binoculars in grandstands up and down the country. 'As each race comes to an end,' he said at today's speech at the

Licenced Turf Accountants Association Annual Luncheon in the grandstand, 'I think to myself, in this day and age, why on earth can't we devise a system in which every horse wins? Why is it just one horse in every race that our society deems to be "the winner"? And why the hell is it never mine?'

4 August 1996

Today our fact-finding mission to Ascot was concentrating on devising a fair and equitable policy for horse-racing under New Labour. Five senior figures – Harriet Harman, Peter Mandelson, John Prescott, Jack Straw and myself – joined Robin Cook and his super long-suffering secretary at Waterloo Station, Jack and Peter in lightweight lounge suits, John Prescott in tail-coat with full gold braid and captain's hat, Harriet and me in the specially designed New Labour Jasper Conran collection of floaty pastel synthetics with its up-to-the-minute emphasis on style over substance.

'Traditionally, this event is known as Royal Ascot, but we in New Labour are not going to be hidebound by tradition. We're determined to change all that nonsense,' observed John Prescott, as our train eased its way into the station.

'I agree with John,' purred Peter Mandelson. '"Royal Ascot" has a harsh, almost unwelcoming tone about it. "Royal Races" or "Royal Fun-Day" would be much more in keeping, don't you think?'

'Could you take everything down in minutes, Miss Regan?' said Robin to his secretary.

'Saucy!' she replied. I wonder what she meant?

5 August 1996

Once inside the course this morning, Peter sped off to sound out ordinary folk about their hopes and dreams for the New Millennium. Peter is a tremendous believer in gathering the representative views of ordinary folk. I had spent the train ride to Ascot this morning reading the case-histories detailed so lovingly in his new book *The Blair Revolution* (Faber, £9.99). Halfway through our on-course picnic, Peter reappeared, thrilled with his vox-pop findings from old people nearby.

'Philip and Elizabeth have been married nearly fifty years,' he began. 'Elizabeth's elderly mum, ninety-six, lives on the same inner-city street but finds it hard to get around much these days. Their eldest son Charles, separated with two kids, has always found it hard to settle down. Seventeen years under this Tory Government has taken its toll on this family unit. Understandably, they desperately want to know what New Labour can offer them.

'So let's take a closer look at their future under Tony Blair. A freshly motivated Social Services sees to it that Elizabeth's old mum gets out to the races twice a week. Philip and Elizabeth may once again bask in the respect of the entire community. And Charles can face the future confident that his talents will be developed under New Labour. Yes – everyone profits under Tony Blair.'

6 August 1996

A bit of a set-to at the paddock today. 'It's an utter disgrace that those horses should be permitted to flout all hygiene regulations by walking round in circles so close to human beings,' barked Jack, his spectacles steaming over in exasperation. 'A New Labour Government will call a halt to these geegee merchants!' Then he went on to survey the race-track with mounting concern. 'This wicked Tory Government has callously allowed this paving to grass over,' he said, 'making it wholly unfit for the elderly and infirm.'

Robin was far away in another world, sizing up the likely winner. 'A little tip in your ear, Bel,' he said to me conspiratorially. 'Always place the same amount of money on every horse in the race – that way you're absolutely bound to win something.'

But Harriet was having none of it. Looking around anxiously, she said, 'I'm not being elitist, but surely in our position we can pay just a little bit extra to someone and they'll tell us which horse is going to come first. Surely that's what true democracy is all about.'

After a lunch of lovely New Labour lobster – and I must say the lobsters looked very well cared for – a great day's racing was crowned by the Blair Handicap, the cup going to the horse that smiled the most and made the sweetest noises.

19 August 1996

All this summer, we have been making great inroads taking our message to the people who really matter, namely the people we wouldn't normally bother with. The week before last, I flew with Glenda Jackson to the beaches of the Costa del Sol to meet all the lovely, lovely ordinary holidaymakers there for full and frank discussions on Gordon Brown's future economic strategy for growth and reinvestment. The plan was for Glenda to act out her super railway-carriage scene in *The Music Lovers*, just to get their attention, then, once she had got it, to launch into a more detailed review of New Labour's plans for reinvigorated financial growth up to and beyond the Millennium.

Shame in a way, but all the lovely holidaymakers must have been planning on an early lunch, as two minutes into Glenda's performance the beach was deserted. But all was not lost: on the flight home, Glenda and I managed to get our two totally great stewardesses very interested in Gordon's plans for a mixed economy, so much so that they took two 'New Labour, New Hope' leaflets away with them, promising to read them if and when they found a window in their hectic schedules. Two potential New Labour votes! Not bad for a day out in Spain! Let's hope the Notting Hill Carnival at the end of the month meets with the same success!

25 August 1996

Wicked totally baadass super day at the Carnival.

It all started in the morning. I turned to my old mate Jack Straw, who had just taken off his lightweight grey suit and was slipping into denims and his old 'Make Love Not War' T-shirt.

'Lively up yourself, Jack,' I said. The New Labour float was standing ready for us all to board. 'And lively up *yourself* too, John!' I said to John Prescott as he removed his distinctive double-breasted jacket and tie and struggled his way into a tie-dye T-shirt, all oranges, mauves and greens, a souvenir of my ex's from the 1974 Reading Festival (topping the bill: Blodwyn Pig).

'Lively up yourselves, lads,' I repeated as John and Jack placed their cardboard electric guitars around their necks, put on their Oasis wigs and false eyebrows, climbed up on to our 'Rockin' New Labour, Rockin' New Hope' float and headed for Ladbroke Grove with Robin Cook on dummy drums. The lovely, lovely Clare Short was a bit silent in her novelty beard and moustache. I guess she was still coming to terms with her new position as Deputy Roadie, having been taken off bass by Tony a fortnight ago – a tough decision, but one widely respected by a cross-section of our litmus groups.

'Notting Hill – here we rockin' come!' I shouted as our float set off from Walworth Road, and with that I switched on the amplifier and the lads started mouthing the words to some of the very best of Bob Marley.

'Dere's gonna be burnin' and lootin' tonii . . . iiight,' mimed Jack Straw as we approached the Vauxhall Bridge in heavy traffic. But then he demanded that the volume be turned down. 'Bel,' he said, his voice going up a monotone, suggesting a fair bit of panic, 'I'm not absolutely sure about these lyrics. Didn't Bob Morley do something more suitable – "Tough on crime, tough on the causes of crime", or something of that sort? After all, he was one of our great English comic actors, and fiercely patriotic to boot!'

'That's *Morley*, Robert *Morley*,' I corrected him. Before Jack could say another word, I turned up the volume. 'I shot the sheriff' boomed out as a young Rastafarian squeegee merchant rushed up to the lorry to wipe our windows. Jack did his level best to keep smiling, bless him.

At Hyde Park Corner, we were joined by Glenda in full regalia from her title role in *Elizabeth R*, fresh from canvassing potential floating voters outside Buckingham Palace. From there, it was full speed ahead to Notting Hill.

'Roots, man!' I shouted.

'Left at the first set of traffic lights, if I'm not much mistaken,' replied Jack.

26 August 1996

Day 2 of the Carnival, and we received a warm Notting Hill-style welcome from all sides of the community. 'Rastaman vibrations yeah – vote for Tony Blair and New Labour,' I announced over the megaphone, while John and Jack and Glenda belted out a totally amazing miming of 'Wonderwall' from the brilliant Oasis. In response, the crowd surged around our float, rocking it to and fro, to and fro before letting down the tyres – a traditional cross-cultural welcome in this most vibrant of communities.

This ensured us a super permanent site at the Carnival for the rest of the afternoon, right up to the moment the RAC managed to break its way through shortly after midnight. Quite unexpectedly, and to our great chuffment, Jack Straw won second prize in the Senior Fancy Dress for coming as Walter from Dennis the Menace. 'But I'm Liam Gallagher!' he protested. But they wouldn't hear a word of it. Yup, New Labour is on its way – jah wobble vibes, y'all!

18 September 1996

A day for thought. Sometimes in the past, I think we in (Old) Labour lost the philosophical arguments, and I'm determined that's not going to happen again. So I sit down and just think and think and think and think. I tell myself we live in an age of unreason, an age of cults and fads and superstitions. It's high time we all pulled ourselves together and behaved like rational human beings. 'Cos for one thing, if we don't live like rational human beings, we'll never ascend to a higher plane in the life to come, and the transmigration of souls could be jeopardised for ever, just as Nostradamus predicted.

Politics is about the here and now, and those of us who are passionate about getting Tony Blair's New Labour into power can't afford to be blown off track by irrational beliefs. That's why Tony's appointed people with their feet well and truly on the ground to the most senior positions in his Shadow Cabinet – three Taureans, one Libran and two Aries, at the last count. This is a mixture that bodes very well for the future, particularly if you take the Islington ley-lines into account.

19 September 1996

Today's meeting of the New Labour steering committee was all about nitty-gritty practicalities: tough decisions for tough times. We sat around the table in Tony's office while the lovely Peter Mandelson (typically Gemini, incidentally) hovered dutifully with the tea and biccies. Top of the agenda was Tony's vision of a Stakeholder Society.

'It's a tremendous vision, absolutely tremendous,' I said to Tony. 'And I'd love to know exactly where you were when you first saw it. Was it in the West Country at all? Glastonbury, Wells, Salisbury Plain – that sort of area?'

Tony tilted his head to one side. I strongly intuited it to be a firm yes from his spirit guide. He then spoke of the Stakeholder Society with real passion. Nobody could prove it was there, he said, because so far it isn't, but that doesn't mean it won't ever be, because it will be if we all believe in it strongly enough.

'But can we be clear exactly what this vision consists of?' said the smashing Gordon Brown – typical Scorpio sceptic, bless him.

'It's a vision of a new tomorrow. A vision of a society in which every man, woman and child shares a vision of a society in which every man, woman and child shares a – now where was I?' replied Tony.

Jack Straw, busy giving his specs the once-over with the baby-wipes, came to the rescue. 'Correct me if I'm wrong, Tony, but you were saying that it is a society in which each and every one of us would be held legally responsible for keeping our own car windscreens clean – thus cutting out those wretched squeegee merchants at the root of their evil monopoly.'

'And you were going on to say that we must extend the frontiers of what I call "caring capitalism",' added Peter, circulating with his tray. 'Take Ron and Ethel, for instance. Ron, 35, is a Pisces and he's been married to Ethel, 43, who is a Taurus, for 20 years. Under the Tories, their chain of garden machinery shops has been greatly reduced. But under New Labour's plans for a Stakeholder Economy, Ron and Ethel's garden machinery flourishes, so much so that they can employ four new managers and a workforce of fifteen. And incidentally Ron will then be able to expand into the sunken-garden business, which he learnt from his time in a previous life tending the hanging gardens of the lost city of Atlantis.'

'Great!' said Tony, wrapping up Item One. Then he moved his hand down the agenda – those hands whose palm clearly states he'll shortly be moving to a location strongly associated with the number '10' – and announced, 'Europe!'

5 October 1996

To the New Labour Party Conference, to make the speech of a lifetime at a fringe meeting organised by the Colour Co-ordination Group. I began in traditional Labour fashion, by sending out Alastair Campbell to find the oldest lady on the streets of Brighton. He managed to rope in three – a fat one, a thin one and an ill one – but I picked the one who looked the most poorly as I wanted to make some very important points about the NHS. At an agreed moment, Alastair bundled the old lady on stage. This allowed me to pay generous tribute to her before an audience teetering on the brink of tears. 'Brenda,' I said, 'you've worked your guts out for the Labour Party these past 73 years. You lost all three children down the asbestos mines and your husband tragically died on the same day the Tories increased the VAT on luxury items. But you never let it get you down. You kept on fighting for New Labour, you kept telling yourself that – yes – one day we'd have a New Labour Prime Minister, who would never ever spend taxpayers' money on unnecessary provisions to those who are a burden on society. And, Brenda, from the bottom of our New Labour hearts, we just want to say thank you. Thank you for keeping the dream alive!'

As I wiped my tears away, Brenda spoke: 'They should never have got rid of Maggie: she did great in the Falklands – and she wouldn't take no nonsense from the blacks neither, and as for those bloody miners . . . !'

'Comrades – a big hand for Brenda!' I interrupted. Alastair bundled her offstage, muting her protests very calmly and caringly through an old chamois leather and a length of sticky-backed plastic.

And so to my speech proper. 'I say this,' I began. 'I love my party. I believe in the family. And let me tell you this. Let me. Tell you. This. I love my country. I love it like I love my party. And my family. And my family in the country. And their party. Everyone's invited. And I will devote every breath I breathe, every sinew of my vortex, to making sure that this party I love remains a part of this country I love.'

I knew I was in the middle of the most powerful and important speech of my political career, and was uniting the party as no one had ever united it, or at least not since Tony's speech the day before.

'Feel New Britain come alive,' I implored, 'feel the vitality course through this country's veins and make it young again. Feel the country reborn. New Britain. New community. New Millennium. New world. New Statesman. New potatoes. New Seekers. New age travellers. New in today. News at Ten. Newton Abbot. Newt Gingrich. New and me baby!'

I had those that remained literally in the palm of my hand. It was time to spell out hard policy. 'I'm not in the business of making promises,' I said, 'but I tell you this. This is what I am telling you. And this is what I have just told you, fairly and squarely. I have said it once, and once only. And now I have said it, let that be an end to it. And that is what I have said. And – my god, isn't it time this Tory Government confronted the problems facing Britain today with the same measure of sound finance, compassion and down-to-earth honesty?' I ended with a flourish. 'Let's never forget what we haven't forgotten – because surely, comrades, that is the only way we'll ever remember.' I sat down in triumph. From where I sat in the Hove Leisure Centre, the way ahead for New Labour had never looked better.

15 October 1996

Believe me, we sang our guts out. That's me and Clare and John and Peter and Barbara and Ken and up to half a million others. You should've heard us. 'So, Sally can't way, She knows it's too lay...' we bellowed, totally without song sheets. 'She da di di da-a a!' You gotta hand it to Noel and Liam; classic rock choruses don't come more memorable than their most famous song, whose name I forget.

Knebworth! The name has a magical ring to it, the 'Kneb' very nearly rhyming with 'Fab', and the 'Worth' not just rhyming with 'worth' but actually *being* 'worth', thus indicating that, as festivals go, this one is always really *worth* it – just so long as there's not a crap band playing.

The memories come flooding back . . . my first Knebworth was the Floyd, back in '77, on their 'Money, it's a Crime' tour, which grossed a record £6 million worldwide, excluding onsite merchandising such as sales of special Pink Floyd 'Money, it's a Crime' pound notes (£1.50) and 'We Don't Need No Education' sweatshirts (£2.50 or £3.50 for the unemployed). It was a time when the Labour Party was beginning to realise the value of reaching out to touch the young, so Fred Mulley and Denis Howell were deputed by Jim Callaghan to 'spread the word' on a special fact-finding mission of Knebworth. The two of them were welcomed onstage by the Floyd, and the rest is history: to background music by Waters and Gilmour and a full light show with state-of-the-art psychedelic bubbles, Mulley read out a two-hour draft discussion document on the future of the Common Fisheries Policy. It proved the most exciting gig the Floyd ever played.

Flash forward to 1983, when the Labour Party and the nation's rock musicians cemented their ties with the formation of Red Wedge. I'm proud to say that my own public relations company, Bel & Frendz, handled all the publicity for this historical grouping, and at its launch at the House of Commons, Roy Hattersley and I accompanied Billy Bragg as he sang:

'England really needs Michael Foot
We don't care whether he wears a donkey jacket or a suit
He'll certainly share out the loot
Let's give Thatcher the boot
It's the working class for who we'll root
Rat-a-tat-tat, Brother, Tooty-toot-toot.'

Powerful stuff. Needless to add, this passionate protest song was an overnight success, rising to number 61 in the charts and contributing much to enabling the Labour Party to sail into another valuable period on the Opposition benches virtually unchallenged.

Thirteen years later, and along come Noel, Liam and the lads to breathe new life into Britpop and new life into New Labour. My good friend, the lovely, lovely Clare Short, turned me on to them. Clare counts herself one of their biggest fans, and has issued a characteristically brave and forthright press release to correct any impression that she isn't.

'My earlier statement that Oasis are "a relentlessly dreary old band of copy-cats and Johnny One-Notes" has been subject to wilful misinterpretation by the Conservative media,' she states. 'I have the greatest respect and admiration for Oasis, particularly their brilliant song "I Wanna Hold Your Hand", which they will begin writing next year.'

And that's how we in New Labour came to make the incredible pilgrimage to Knebworth. If Oasis can win over the hearts and minds of the British people, then so can New Labour – and we want to find out exactly how to go about it.

Peter Mandelson wrapped up well: he's been getting a little chilly ever since he lent his moustache to Noel Gallagher for use as a pair of winter eyebrows. The Folletts made great efforts to be entirely democratic by hiring an extra coach for their household staff, the price of their tickets to be set against the completion of the requisite number of kitchen chores. And Clare, of course, sang her guts out, only once or twice having to alter her lyrics after a swift but gentle kick in the shins from Peter. 'So, Sally can't wait,' she crooned, 'she knows it's too late. In fact, it's not too late, and actually I wholly agree with Sally that she can wait as long as she likes, da da di da-a-a'. Magic! Da da di da-a-a! That's a vision of New Labour that, just this once, we can all share in.

12 November 1996

'Am I right, or am I right,' asked the lovely Johnny Prescott, 'or is the weather getting one helluva lot worse under the present iniquitous and wholly discredited Tory Government? It's pelting outside, and here's me in me Hush Puppies, and the tasselled ones at that, dammit.'

We were in an emergency session of the George Brown Group, the top-secret New Labour intellectual think-tank that meets every third Tuesday, ideas permitting. In the light of the potentially ruinous upturn in our economy, Tony – bless him – had been keen that we in New Labour should come up with some smashing new ideas.

'Snow in November!' sighed Harriet H, with a smile. 'Can't wait for our fortnight in our fave hotel in the Bahamas!' Call me superstitious, but I could have sworn I heard a pin drop. Tony took the opportunity to shuffle his papers. Robin Cook pulled vigorously at his beard. Jack Straw cleared his throat, leaving the polished table in need of a squeegee merchant.

But Harriet soon corrected herself. 'Charter flight, of course,' she said. 'Self-catering. And fact-finding too. I'd much prefer Eastbourne – no, Blackpool – but it's completely chocker. And we prefer to mix with a majority ethnic population. We can learn so much from them. Have you seen them dance? Tremendous rhythm.'

'Thank you for that contribution, Harriet,' said Tony, our Chair. 'If we could return to the weather, I personally find it abhorrent that in a so-called democratic country you cannot open your window at night for fear of rain coming in. Only yesterday, our new rattan carpet – fashionable, maybe, but hard-wearing with it – was literally *soaked*. But do we have the statistics on hand to back up my gut reaction that this weather we're having is a Tory problem, created by the Tories, fostered by the Tories and – let's face it, chums – the blame for which must be laid fairly and squarely at the door of the Tories?'

'May I interject, Tony?' said Peter Mandelson, who's been feeling the cold ever since he took the brave decision to shave off his moustache two years ago come March. 'I see a poster campaign developing. I see big, I see bold, I see full colour, I see twelve hundred key sites, up and down the country. An Arctic landscape – ice, igloos, polar-bears, the lot – and, underneath, the simple slogan 'Life's Colder Under Major'.

There was a stunned silence. I guess we all knew we were privileged to be present at the birth of a great new idea, just like they must have felt at Hiroshima. 'Love it,' said Tony, adding, 'but the Tories are bound to trot out their tired old question "So what would you guys do instead?"'

'Fair point, Tony,' said Jack Straw, removing his specs and giving them a good polish with his tie, a sure sign his brain is ticking over. 'And I think we can hit them with a three-point agenda. May I present it in outline?'

'Fire away, Jack,' said Tony, ever-keen to entertain new ideas, just so long as they're fresh and appealing.

'One. New Labour will attempt to undo the damage done by eighteen untold years of Tory misrule. Two. New Labour will initiate immediate on-the-spot fines for those who persistently refuse to go out without their waterproofs on. Three. Parents of children who splash around in puddles quite regardless of the effect it will have on the dampness or otherwise of the trousers and/or skirts of themselves and/or others will face a preliminary caution followed by a custodial sentence as and when appropriate.'

'But surely we must tackle this problem at source?' chipped in the super David Blunkett. 'As I see it, it's primarily a question of teaching our young folk to be weather-wise – a vital part of our education system sorely neglected by this wicked Tory Government. Kids these days can leave school without realising that the colder it is, the more winter woollies they should put on. And vice versa. Last August, there were lads in my constituency walking round in thick polo-necks, double-vests, donkey-jackets and thermal underwear when it was a hundred degrees in the shade. That's Tory education policy for you!'

'Thanks, David, for that moving speech,' said Tony, dabbing at his eyes with a handkerchief. 'Anything further to add, Bel?'

'Let's launch a 24-hour Weather Clothes Lines,' I suggested, 'so that all our folk, young and senior, can be given up-to-the-minute advice on suitable outdoor wear for the prevailing weather conditions. It would make a great photo-op, perhaps with Gordon Brown standing under a shower with an umbrella, giving us the thumbs-up.'

'Lubbly jubbly,' said John Prescott, wrapping up the meeting. 'New Labour is now firmly established as the natural Party of Weather. Yup, it sure looks like we've turned out nice again . . .'

28 November 1996

There's nothing I love more than sitting round a table with some good mates grappling with current affairs. At a Hammersmith café run by Ruthie Rogers, I was discussing Barbie Dolls with my good friends Harriet Harman and Barbara Follett, bless 'em. We all breathed huge sighs of relief that somehow we had avoided Barbie's pernicious influence.

'One thing I totally detest about the Talking Barbie,' said Harriet, 'is the way you pull her cord and she just trots out the same tired old slogans. It's tired old slogans, tired old slogans, all the time tired old slogans. Yup, that's what I really hate about the Talking Barbie – the endless repetition of tired old slogans. If it's not one tired old slogan, do you know what it is? It's another tired old slogan. One tired old slogan after another. And basically I'm sick to death of tired old . . .'

'And though it might not affect us,' butted in Barbara, looking utterly brilliant in a vivid-red teamed costume with pillbox-hat and matching stilettos, topped off with a marvellously brave shade of bright scarlet lipstick, 'because let's face it, we three are at the forefront of feminist thought, some of my little constituents, poor loves, honestly think that their lives will be made happier if they act "the little woman" and spend far more than they should on clothes, make-up and fashion accessories.' And with that Barbara threw her brand-new little black Chanel bag down on the table in a show of defiance against the system.

'But we can't just sit here doing nothing. As women, we must take the matter into our own hands,' I announced. 'Remember what Tony says? He says, "New Labour, new solutions".' I then reminded Harriet and Barbara that, nurturing my son Marley in the 1970s, I totally opposed providing him with toy weapons or war games of any sort. Marley never had any need of Action Man, I told them. Why should he? I preferred to foster his interest in the environment and the living, breathing, hope-filled world around him. Okay, so he went through a tough time as a teenager, twice being cautioned by police after bludgeoning a senior citizen with a sharpened cucumber. But since then the boy's shed one helluva lot of anger: he assures me that the message of his band's latest rap, 'Stab 'n' Kik Yo' Face In', is basically about vegetarianism, if you read between the lines.

4 December 1996

Another profitable head-banging session with Harriet and Barbara! Knowing that by discouraging war games for our sons we are promoting a more loving and peace-filled society, shouldn't we also discourage gender-stereotyping dolls for our daughters? 'What we really need,' agreed Harriet, 'is an enlightened toy manufacturer to come up with some great new positive dolls for the 1990s. New Labour – new dolls.'

There and then, we ordered another three spritzers and began chewing on our Berols. Who was the real new Action Man for the 1990s, a suitable role-model for the caring guys of tomorrow? We thought long and hard but were getting nowhere until who should walk by – ('Hi, ladies, hmmmmm, those spritzers certainly look good: can I join you?') – but our good friend Mr Jack Straw.

Then it hit me! Because the Shadow Home Secretary and I have been very close buddies since our Leeds University days (we used to read the lyrics of *Teaser and the Firecat* out loud together), I didn't want to be the first to put his name forward. But out of nowhere Barbara said, 'I've got it! The Jack Straw Doll, plus spectacle case and sensible suit! A role-model the young men of tomorrow can really believe in!'

If all goes according to plan, Hornby Toys will be manufacturing an eleven-inch scale model of Jack Straw, complete with adjustable spectacles, ready for distribution in autumn 1997. Youngsters will be able to change him in and out of a choice of lightweight suits, ready to do battle with his deadly enemies The Squeegee Merchants. But The Jack Straw will be an Action Man with a difference: the only weapons he'll employ will be the weapons of rhetoric and logic. Pull up his shirt, pull the string on his back, and he'll say, 'Tough on crime, tough on the causes of crime.' Pull it again, and he'll say, 'Shouldn't you be in bed by now, young man? Police! Police!' One further pull, and he'll refer you to a reply he gave earlier. Wicked!

25 December 1996

Happy Christmas? Hardly. So what happened? My bloke gave me scarlet suspenders and matching stockings. I couldn't believe it – and after I'd written a major article in the *Observer* only last Sunday condemning men who see their women solely as sex-objects with gifts of wholly inappropriate lingerie! After repeated cross-questioning it emerged that he hadn't bothered to read the article – not even once.

Something on the sports pages, he said, had 'caught his eye'. What? 'Wrestling.' Wrestling? I couldn't believe it. The times I've argued – forcefully, cogently, without losing my cool – that wrestling is a barbaric activity full of male testosterone, a sport (so-called!) that would be banned in any halfway civilised country – and yet here he is, saying he's neglected my seminal psychological insights for a piece on wrestling!

But you're not even interested in wrestling, I pointed out. 'I'm not,' he said, 'I got it wrong. I thought it was women's all-in mud-wrestling.'

We split up at 10.12 a.m. precisely. I don't expect to see him again. 'Nuff said. Good riddance. His wife's welcome to him – and so are the electorate. And I'm never going to confide who he is, not even to this diary. He's just not worth it, and I don't care if he *is* a senior Cabinet Minister with red hair and a beard, damn him.

26 December 1996

Noon. The doorbell goes. I wipe away the tears, tidy myself up. ''Tis the season to be merry, tra-la-la-la-la-la la-la-la, *sob*.' It's the Folletts – Ken and Barbara – at the door, full of seasonal merriment, with Barbara looking fantastic, all in red with white fluffy ribbing – a costume she hasn't worn since her days as a member of the Younger Generation on the Cliff Richard Christmas Special in December 1973.

'Come in, come in!' I choked. 'Robin's – er – not – going to be able to – er – make it – er – sadly. But the others will all be here in a sec. Orange or Diet Coke? Or something stronger, just so long as you're not driving?'

The Folletts made themselves at home, Barbara talking Ken through the 15-second solo (arms out, arms in, cheeky wink, run towards the camera smiling, veer away at last moment, still smiling) she performed in the 'Would you like to ride in my beautiful, my beautiful ball-oo-oo-oo-oon' Younger Generation routine back in 1972. 'And 15 seconds was a lot of time in those days,' she reminded us.

'Great training for the General Election,' I agreed. At that moment – just as Ken was picking up his electric guitar to move us all with his version of 'Knockin' On Heaven's Door', the doorbell rang. It was the lovely Harriet Harman, plus my old mate Jack Straw and a very festive-looking Peter Mandelson, wearing a snowy muff to keep his hands from the winter chill. Few people realise how thoughtful Peter is. 'I've told my chauffeur he can listen to the car radio while he waits. After all, it is Christmas, and we are New Labour,' he explained, kindly.

Still struggling to come to terms with the traumatic personal events of yesterday, desperate to divert my very special guests from my own very real festive tragedy, I directed them all to my Christmas crib, complete with Mary, Joseph, Infant, Shepherds, Wise Men and livestock.

'That's a perfect cross-section you've got there, Bel,' said Peter. 'The mother, child and common-law husband would be at least £2.50 a week better off under New Labour, the farm labourers would benefit from the EC minimum wage, the Wise Men would be welcomed to a central advisory body, and only the livestock would have to be put down.'

Jack was a little concerned. 'Should that infant really be up so late? Parents must be taught responsibility for their children's actions. And that crib is a health-hazard. It certainly wouldn't comply with household hygiene regulations under a New Labour Government.'

18 January 1997

Will the strains in our lovely New Labour friendships hold up until after the Election? It was a question that was worrying me all through dinner with the lovely John Prescott. Like many who are absolutely right behind Tony in his leadership of New Labour, I have one helluva lot of time for John. He may not talk like the rest of us, and he may never have been to the 1969 Isle of Wight Festival armed with just a pair of bongos and a whole lotta love. But so bloody what? He is the representative of the working class in Tony's Shadow Cabinet, a constant reminder to the rest of us of the very real roots of the Old Labour Party, and how they continue to grow beneath the floor of our super New Labour house.

Actually, there's an interesting sidelight on all this. In that heady summer of love, John just happened to be the chief steward aboard the Isle of Wight ferry that transported all us assorted heads and freaks to the festival. Jack Straw and I were an 'item' at the time (Jack was the assistant flautist in Tir na Nog, I played occasional castanets with Hawkwind) and we travelled on that ferry with Mike Meacher, who helped out on triangle with the Edgar Broughton Band, Tony Blair, who was heavily into Roger Whittaker, and Margaret Beckett, who was at that time hotly tipped as Hartlepool's answer to Joan Baez. I suppose we may have had a spliff or two, because just as we were halfway through our journey and Mike Meacher was yelling his heart out to the latest Joni Mitchell ('We are STARDUST, We are GOLDEN!'), Jack Straw had a brilliant idea.

'Let's turn on the fuzz,' he said. 'I mean, they're people like us, they're beautiful too, they don't have to be pigs, no way, we gotta liberate them.'

At that time a man in full dress uniform with a badge saying Chief Petty Steward Prescott walked past. Jack sprang to his feet and rushed over to Chief Petty Steward Prescott. 'We love you, man,' he said, and presented him with a daffodil.

The Chief Petty Steward held it in his left hand, looked at it, and pulled its head off. 'Plants and livestock to be kept in the hold, sir,' he said through gritted teeth. 'Offenders may face prosecution. If you'll excuse me, some of us have a job to do.'

It was more than ten years later that Jack first found his way into Parliament. By now he was sporting short hair and heavy spectacles. By an amazing coincidence, on his very first day he bumped into his fellow MP John Prescott. He held out his hand in greeting, but John rebuffed him. 'You know something, mush?' said John. 'I never forget a face.' And ever since that day, their relationship has never been what I call truly warm. Frankly, it didn't surprise me when Jack wasn't there tonight, bless him.

11 February 1997

It's been a day to remind me that I am still as young and idealistic and angry and *vibrant* as I was twenty years ago. It took me back to the days of punk. And I was there at the birth. Even twenty years ago I could tell that songs like 'No Future' had an amazing future.

I take a schlepp down memory lane, back twenty years to the days when Sid and Johnny and the rest of that defiant crew were shaking their fists at the class-ridden social conditions into which they had been environmentalised. You knew it was for real, and sure enough three years later as a result of the Pistols' mould-breaking songs, the whole rotten Tory Government came crashing down. Or at least it would have done if it had been a Tory Government. Instead, it was a Labour Government which came crushing down, and it was Welcome to Thatcher's Britain – making the Pistols' songs such as 'Fascist Regime' all the more prophetic.

Like many other people, I was just past my early-to-late twenties at the time, and I was angry as hell. God, was I angry. I remember seeing a can in the street, and just kicking it without caring who saw me. Another time, I bought a great big safety pin, stuck it any-old-how on a shirt and then wore it angrily around the house. Once in the car my mates and I all sang 'God save the Queen/A fascist regime/Gotta let off a bit of steam' all the way back to Cheam at the very tops of our voices, only lowering the volume when passing through built-up areas.

And my generation never ever lost that rage, that burning desire for revolution. Many of the names we now associate with the Blair revolution were in fact early followers of punk. As is widely known, Jack Straw was a founding member of The Damned, only they got rid of him when Rat Scabies decided as part of their overall music policy they didn't want a washboard. So Jack joined New Labour instead, in search of something more mellow.

But take it from me, Jack remains a punk at heart. Today, I

saw him seething with such real anger that he even began quoting from Johnny Rotten. Jack was driving me to Walworth Road for an urgent meeting when the lights turned red.

'Come on, come on,' he muttered through clenched teeth, tapping on the steering-wheel of his Volvo saloon with mounting rage.

At that point, two youths appeared, one with a bucket of water, the other with a wiper.

'Bloody hell!' yelled Jack. 'It's those damned squeegee merchants again! Talk about "fascist regime"!' The lights went green, and we managed to drive off without surrendering our principles or our money. But the incident made me think.

'You must channel that anger, Jack!' I implored him. 'You must be sure those punk ideals we once nurtured never, ever die! You must turn that anger into something relevant, something that can truly change this country of ours! You must form a New Labour Policy (Squeegee Prohibition) Group!'

As you can imagine, there were tears in our eyes. And Jack really did learn to channel that anger of his: he has now privately promised that the very first act of an incoming New Labour Government will be the introduction of tougher sentencing for squeegee merchants, with up to five years detention for a first offence, and life for offences committed thereafter. So our old ideals are not dead. Let's boogie!

3 March 1997

A great night out for Tony. A great night out for New Labour. And a great night out for Britain. Yup, it was this year's Brit Awards, that literally incredible celebration of the new explosion of British youth and talent. 'I live in a house in a very big house in the countraaaaay,' sang Blur, and you felt your whole body rising up, and not just because it was nearly time to go.

All of us in New Labour felt it would be fantastic to forge an association with youth and optimism, so Donald Dewar was put in charge of booking a table way back in December. The eight of us – Donald (wearing flared jeans in memory of his days on bass in The Groundhogs), the lovely Ken and Barbara Follett, Tony, me, Jack Straw (looking very casual in a cravat over a beige polo-neck), Margaret Beckett (ex-Steeleye Span) and John Prescott squeezed into his loon-pants – were lucky enough to share a table with the super young lads from Oasis.

Over dinner, we were keen to find out what the youth of Britain really thinks about the major issues confronting this country. Over soup, Margaret, sitting next to Noel Gallagher, suggested perhaps we might harness the great energy of Britpop to help solve some of the problems facing us. Noel brought the natural verve of youth to his reply. 'Piss off, Toothy,' he said, reaching for another can of lager.

'Thanks, Noel. I certainly think that response gives us much to build on,' enthused Tony. 'Any other suggestions, lads?'

At this point, the Oasis drummer removed Jack Straw's specs and began to wiggle them round in the air with all the super high spirits of the young. Jack made it clear he was enjoying the joke tremendously by laughing for five-to-six seconds before saying, 'Joke over, lads – joke over.' But by this time the drummer had given them to the rhythm guitarist, who was now wearing them on his bottom.

'Are New Labour's plans for the re-nationalisation of our railways exciting much interest among the young?' asked John Prescott.

'Speak up, Fatty!' replied Liam Gallagher, and we all laughed appreciatively at his rough-and-ready Scouse wit while he amiably sprayed us all with a frothed-up can of Carlsberg Special Brew.

As you know, Tony has always been a terrific fan of pop music, and for much of the first session – by the exciting new band Blur – I noted he had his top set of teeth pressed over his bottom lip while his hands played along on his dummy guitar. Meanwhile, Jack Straw was busily trying to retrieve his spectacles, which by now had been passed by the rhythm guitarist to the bass guitarist from Garbage, who had used his lighter to bend them into some sort of abstract 'mound', reflecting the spiritual aspirations of the young.

'I live in a house, a very big house, in the countraaaaay,' sang Blur in the next set. I noticed that Margaret, having removed her straw hat with its green ribbon, had got out her pocket calculator to work out how the aforementioned very big house in the country would be affected from a tax point of view under New Labour, if it was owner-occupied with a fifty per cent endowment mortgage, repayable over twenty-five years. 'Best not tell him,' she whispered to me, 'but he'll be seven per cent worse off under New Labour.'

Next came Tony's big moment. He was presenting the Lifetime Achievement award to David Bowie. Tony was wearing his loose-cut Armani dark suit with a floral tie, but beneath it – and this is what the viewers couldn't see – he was kitted out in a multi-coloured Aladdin Sane body-stocking, ready to meet his hero.

'It's been a great year of energy, youth, vitality, and great, great music,' began Tony, 'and, believe me, we in New Labour draw terrific inspiration from your tremendous efforts.' Sadly, the rest of his speech was drowned out for me by the organist from Screwball vomiting over Ken Follett's double-breasted suit.

25 March 1997

Election fever is hotting up. And after a thousand years The House of Lords is beginning to realise that we're totally committed to getting real. About bloody time too. Jack Straw has already submitted his proposals for the reform of the Upper House. 'We've had enough of all this nonsense about titles, Bel,' he told me this morning, 'so we'll have no hesitation in abolishing them. That's after the usual process of reports, discussion documents, weekend conferences, memos and round-table discussions. We don't want to leap into anything this unconventional without due caution. True radicals, Bel, should never stray far off the beaten track.'

'So there won't be any Lords and Ladies by the time we're senior citizens, then, Jack,' I asked.

Jack looked up. 'Not nearly so many, Bel,' he replied, 'but on the other hand we'll have to make special provision so that people of proven quality – senior citizens of exceptional ability with something to contribute to the community – can still have a forum.'

'People like . . . well . . . you and me, Jack?'

'Well illustrated, Bel.'

'And would we be called – for example – Lord Straw and Lady Littlejohn? Would we, Jack?'

'Well, it's dangerous to break with all tradition in one fell swoop, isn't it? There must always be a period of transition, Bel. Time to take stock and all that.'

'That's so true, Jack – as Tony himself always says, "Change is gonna come – so for God's sake let's not rush it." And, Jack, I suppose we'd still be forced to wear those ermine robes, wouldn't we?'

'Yes, Bel – but only as a symbol of our solidarity with the ordinary working people of this country.'

'That's such a beautiful sentiment, Jack. I must remember to tell Melvyn in the morning,' I replied, 'or Lord Bragg, as we'll have to get used to calling him, poor thing.'

9 April 1997

To the launch of the New Labour manifesto. Disappointed? Just a bit. Disappointed for the lovely Jack Straw, rather than for myself, I mean. After all those years of ceaseless campaigning, there's still not a word in it about the squeegee merchants.

Jack was a wee bit hurt. Of course he was. Who wouldn't be? From private soundings, he'd been persuaded that severe penalties for the squeegee merchants – say, five years for anyone caught with a chamois leather, seven for a sponge and a bucket – were on the cards. He had even posed for a huge hoarding showing him leaping out of his car and taking off his glasses before making a citizen's arrest of two youths with buckets. The slogan? 'New Labour – Stamping Out the Squeegees'. But then disaster struck. It wasn't in.

'I want to put your squeegee merchants on the back-burner,' Tony had said, over a working breakfast.

'Torture, you mean?' Jack had replied, excitedly. But Tony wasn't having it. He said he wanted to emphasise New Labour's more caring approach towards vehicle cleanliness.

Jack rang me, gutted, choking back the tears, bless him. 'Bel,' he says, 'Bel, I've got to look my best for the launch. Could you come and give me a makeover?'

Luckily, I had the lovely Barbara Follett with me. Together we nipped to New Labour HQ. Frankly, Jack was looking dreadful, his hair all over the place, Jimi Hendrix style, his spectacles steaming, his mouth locked in a dreadful grimace. 'I'm so upset about the manifesto, but I must look lovely for the launch, girls. Please – give me a makeover,' he implored.

It takes guts for a man to express his inner pain. 'Let it out, Jack!' I begged, and while he sobbed and sobbed Barbara and I checked out the New Labour guidelines for makeover tips for candidates. Point One on the checklist was 'avoid untidy hairstyles or hair in face', so I gave his hair a thorough going over. I've always thought Martyn Lewis on the BBC has very clean, neat, well-groomed hair, so I'd brought along a photograph. So far so good. But then it came to Jack's face, drawn and dishevelled. It needed a thorough wash.

'You know what we really really want for your face? A squeegee merchant!' I joked.

'That's it. I'm off!' said Jack. But at this point the door to the dressing room flew open.

'Ladies and gentlemen, this is your five-minute call!' It was Peter Mandelson, very chirpy till he set eyes on Jack. 'You're not planning to wear those to the manifesto launch?'

he gasped, pointing at Jack in his 'Hom for Men' Y-fronts and string vest. 'You can't launch a manifesto in your underwear, it'll send out the wrong message!'

'Can't you see the poor guy's upset?' I snapped, as Barbara got out the blusher and foundation and set to work on Jack's face.

'And can't he do something about those simply dreadful glasses? They're so . . . severe,' barked Peter. Something told me he was rattled. 'But I'm not going to stand around chatting all day, I've got to check Robin's sorted out his eyeliner and done something about that ghastly beard. If Jack doesn't want to be Home Secretary, it's not my fault.' And with that he slammed the door.

With two minutes to go, Jack emerged as spruce as ever, looking great in the warm, confident smile Barbara had given him with a few deft dabs of the Max Factor.

19 April 1997

And good riddance! Only another two weeks to go, and we'll be rid of this elitist Tory Government for ever, with their gongs and privileges and their jobs for the boys. Time then for those of us who know Tony, who believe in Tony, who value Tony as a close personal friend, to step forward and lend the guy a helping hand.

21 April 1997

Victory seems assured. I'm proud to count myself a close personal friend of New Labour, one who's slogged her guts out under the elitist Tory jackboot of £100-a-head dinners these past five years. I didn't do it for myself. But I know that Tony, bless him, won't want to forget a dear old friend and influential commentator when he finally pushes open that door to Number 10.

I first met Tony at a *Guardian* lunch in 1989. At one point I passed him the salt, and I specifically remember asking him whether he'd like some more carrots, which he was extremely grateful to accept. That was when I learnt that Tony really loves carrots, they're one of his favourite vegetables. I'll never forget the way he ate them – first cutting them neatly then prodding them sincerely with his fork, and finally placing them in his mouth, chewing them and swallowing them with statesmanlike charm. Even then, I could tell that this was one guy who was going to go far. Now whenever journalists are writing profiles of Tony, they'll always ring me to check exactly what his favourite vegetables are, and exactly how he eats them. And even if I'm snowed under with work, I'll do my best to oblige: anything to assure victory for New Labour.

Since then, we've kept bumping into one another at functions, including last month's £500-a-head brunch for New Labour thrown by Ruthie Rogers and Barbara Follett. I was sitting at a table with some other women very important to New Labour, including a former deputy editor of *TV Quick* magazine and a news announcer from Radio 5. I could see Tony getting a touch bored with his table – mainly rather earnest and unfashionably dressed MPs and trade unionists, most of them 'sons of toil' and (forgive me!) a little bit awkward at these stylish events – so I scribbled a note on my menu telling him where I was sitting, reminding him of our past encounters, letting him know I was a good friend of Jack Straw and informing him that I had one or two exciting new ideas up my sleeve to help lower taxation for the achievers in our society.

I could tell he was interested by the way he scrutinised it before resuming his conversation with the trade unionist to his right. On the way out, I greeted him like a long-lost friend. 'Tony!' I said. 'Bel Littlejohn. We must stop meeting like this! I've got some great thoughts for New Labour I'd like to share with you. When would be convenient? And – do tell – how are Cherie and the kids? Great!'

27 April 1997

Bridge-building is what New Labour is all about. I'll do anything to build a bridge between Number 10 and my own front door. Obviously I don't expect to be a guest at Tony and Cherie's At Home on 2 May. They'll have far too many *apparatchiks*, middle-rankers, deputy leaders and 'party workers' to work through over beer or house wine. But after a while they'll be able to enjoy more relaxed gatherings with dear friends and, no doubt, the odd bottle of vintage bubbly. So I imagine I'll be invited around to Downing Street before the month of May is over, first for a celebration glass, then for ongoing discussions on my role, if any, in the New Labour administration. It'll be just the time when he really needs us, time for those of us who know Tony, who believe in Tony, and who value Tony as a close personal friend to lend the guy a helping hand. Here's a promise. When Tony and Cherie move into 10 Downing Street, Bel Littlejohn will be behind them every step of the way.

28 April 1997

Tony is a great judge of character; I guess that's why he likes me. He knows I'm not one of those who hanker after power and its trappings. He knows I'd continue to count on me as his good friend and political ally even if he fails to gain power on 1 May and is thrust back into obscurity. Though obviously he understands that our paths wouldn't cross so frequently, and his replacement as Leader of New Labour would have a right to expect my undivided loyalty and, sadly, what with one thing and another, we'd be almost bound to lose touch for years on end.

But for the time being, let's concentrate on scoring our own goals. Let's kick out this wholly corrupt Tory Government, its backhanders, its backscratching, its ruthless defence of its own privileges. We've had it up to here with empty slogans. Britain deserves better. Then – and only then – will we, the friends of Tony and Cherie, be able to take up our rightful places in the drawing room of Number 10. Let's go, gang!

2 May 1997

I don't mind admitting it: I cried. Yup: she cried; he cried; you cried; they cried; we all cried. Tears of joy; tears of hope; tears of sorrow for seventeen long, wasted years. But above all the tears of sweet, sweet victory.

Labour gain. Labour gain. Labour gain. Those two little words, repeated so often through the night, said it all. Suddenly, the country seemed new and young and vibrant. Overnight, it had swapped a pinstripe suit for a pair of well-pressed flares and a tie-dye T-shirt. Overnight, we had become a more compassionate, caring, forgiving society, unafraid of showing our emotions. And, God, didn't we all like watching that look on Portillo's face when he knew he'd lost? Didn't we just want to grind his face down into the dirt and see him squeal with humiliation! And you know what? I think he almost cried! Yes – cried! I got up close to my television screen and looked hard into his eyes. And I nearly saw a tear! Yes! A grown man blubbing! Ha! So much for him!

Suddenly, the air seems different, so very different. People are walking up to total strangers in the street and telling them they care. 'It's a beautiful noise,' wrote Neil Diamond a few short years ago, 'comin' up from the street.' And he might well have been talking about the mood in Britain today. 'Rejoice!' the very birds in the air seem to chirrup, 'Rejoice! Rejoice!'

My predictions for the first year of Tony's new government? First I'll list a few things I can guarantee a New Labour Government *won't* be doing.

After seventeen years of Tory seediness, there *won't* be the relentless sex scandals of recent years. There'll be an end to broken marriages, an end to senior ministers cheating on

226

their loyal wives – and certainly an end to that peculiarly Tory speciality of ministers having it off with their so-called 'secretaries', and I employ the phrase lightly, while their long-suffering wives are fighting their corner back in the constituency. When you've got guys in the Cabinet of the moral force and sheer personal integrity of, say, Robin Cook, you just know that, as the poet said, the times they are a-changin'.

This Government *won't* be throwing the hard-earned money of the people away on self-aggrandising schemes and monuments. When you think of the literally thousands of pounds Lady Thatcher spent on those fancy new gates for Downing Street, you can be sure that New Labour has learnt its lesson. Tony isn't into all this 'international prestige' nonsense. Budgets spent on government houses will be ruthlessly pared down, so that if, say, a Labour minister wants to redecorate his home, he'll have to dip into his own pocket for all the basics from B&Q. And now that a truly down-to-earth bloke like John Prescott has his hands on the driving seat, the self-glorifying Conservative Millennium Dome of Heseltine *et al* will disappear into the furthest reaches of our memory, the money saved spent on hospitals and schools.

There *won't* be any kow-towing to vested interests. Unlike the Tory Party, we in New Labour have no time for million-pound secret 'donations' (note the quote marks!!) from the Fat Cats of big business. And no longer will we be the lap-dogs of America: never again will we fight America's wars, never again will we act as her dumping ground for the nuclear waste nobody else will take. Nor will we let Murdoch extend his wicked empire an inch further – and if that means losing the support of his so-called newspapers, so be it.

And what *will* we have accomplished within the first year of a New Labour Government? Shorter hospital waiting lists. A better deal for teachers. More open government, with no more press officers coming between us and our representatives. A Cabinet composed of friendly colleagues, all fighting for the common cause. An end to the politics of sound-bites. C'mon, everybody! Brush away those tears! As the late, great Bob Marley so prophetically said, 'Everything's gonna be all right.' Rejoice! Rejoice! Rejoice!

Appendix 1

Tony Blair's introduction to the New Labour Election Manifesto 1997
(*written for him by Bel Littlejohn*)

I believe in Britain. Great! It's a great country with a great history. Great! The British people are a great people. You feel great and I feel great. We all feel great. Everything's really great.

On second thoughts, under the Conservatives it's not so great after all. In fact, it could be a lot greater.

I want a Britain that is one nation, with shared values and purpose.

A Britain where everyone is happy and carefree and no one is upset.

A modern, go-ahead Britain, where folk are able to walk down the street and reach their destinations on time.

A Britain that can hold its head high and is proud to wear the very latest fashions as it swaggers along to a dinner-date with a delightful friend.

I want a Britain that does not shuffle into the New Millennium afraid of the future. I want a Britain that strides into the future with a sense of purpose, hogging a seat near the front, maximising the elbow-room for itself.

I want a Britain we can all feel part of. I want a Britain in which what I want for my own children is what I want for yours – but only after I have got it for mine. I want a Britain free of queue-barging.

We have modernised the Labour Party and we will modernise Britain. Let me give you an example. Do you remember John Prescott five years ago? John will be the first to agree that he looked drab, overweight, outdated – a real no-hoper. But look at him, now: wearing smart, double-breasted suits, every bit the city gent. Under New Labour, everyone will look as modern as John Prescott.

The difference between us and the Conservatives is that we know where we want to go. We want to go forwards. And we know how to get there. Straight on. Right a bit. Left a bit. Stop. And then ask.

We will *promote personal prosperity for all*.

We as a nation must face up to some harsh truths. We in New Labour recognise that success is better than abject failure.

Happiness is better than downright misery.

Children are a precious asset.

Too many cooks spoil the broth.

More hands make light work.

It's a long way to Tipperary.

A room decorated entirely in grey can be said to lack colour.

There is nothing worse than a ballpoint pen bursting in the top pocket of a white jacket.

And cash in the pocket is better than cash in the hand – because that way you don't lose it.

I'm not saying the process by which we arrived at these conclusions has not been long and – at times – painful. But I believe we have made them in the best interests of the ordinary men and women of this country of ours.

We have done nothing more and nothing less than set out to establish a new trust for a new deal for a new partnership for a new approach for a new spirit for a new contract with the British people for the New Millennium.

It's as simple as that.

A new trust. A new deal. A new partnership. A new approach. A new spirit. A new contract. A New Millennium.

And together the seven of them – four in the back, three in the front, driven by the new deal, with the new contract reading the map and the new spirit barking out directions – will set off to the land of the future. But only after they have all taken advantage of the facilities. For let me assure them of one thing. There'll be no stopping along the way.

We will *make everyone much more healthy*.

Over nineteen years of Conservative rule, many millions of people have died.

Particularly the elderly and infirm.

The cause? Ill-health.

Let's make no bones about it. Ill-health is a major cause of death in our society.

And we will attack the root causes of ill-health. We will set up a major network of new initiative zones to tackle the long-term problems of expanding perceptions among the elderly and the infirm.

Under New Labour, the people of Britain will no longer feel ill. Instead, they will be encouraged to feel that their bodies have instituted major new initiatives to combat on-going functions. Under New Labour, the people of Britain will no longer die. Instead, they will be able to feel that a complete re-evaluation of facilities has resulted in an exciting new programme of bodily decommissioning.

We will *give as good as we get*.

What we've got is good. But we've got to get what we've got and give what we get to know that what we've got is as good as what we get. Frankly, what's the good of getting as good as what we've got if we can't give as good as we get?

Any decision about a single currency must be determined by hard-headed assessment of Britain's best economic interests.

It is quite clear what we must do.

We must either go in.

Or we must stay out.

Only New Labour can be trusted to make the one choice.

Or the other.

But we make this solemn pledge.
We will never make both choices.
Unless circumstances are right.
New Labour. Because Britain deserves better.
Or roughly the same.

Appendix 2

Prime Minister Tony Blair's speech to the Labour Party Conference 1998 (*from an original draft by Bel Littlejohn*)

Look, I believe in Britain. I believe in the British people. One cross on the ballot paper, one nation was reborn. Today, I want to set an ambitious course for this country: a course for change.

Look, the British don't fear change. Far from it. All over this nation of ours, people are crying out for it. Only this morning, on the way into the Conference a young fellow looked me in the eye and cried out, 'Any change, guv?'

And let me tell you this. I told him that I had some hard choices to make. And make them I most certainly would. I told him I wasn't going to be rushed into making this hard choice. But I made this solemn promise to that young man: when the time comes to make a hard choice, I will make the hardest choice of all.

And – do you know? – I think he smiled.

Look, I want Britain to be a nation where we learn the lessons of British industrial relations over the past hundred years. I say this to workers and trade unionists: you deserve a bigger share of profits, a more powerful voice on the shop-floor, greater consultation over the way ahead.

And I say to small businessmen and industrialists this: ignore what I've just said to them. For all their bleatings and complainings and excessive wage demands, it's your side I'm really on.

And I say to middle-management and those caught somewhere between the two: believe me, they're both as bad as each other, let's sort them both out, so that the ordinary, decent Britons like us can at last enjoy the fruits of our labours.

We want flexibility. The flexibility of an elastic band. Just imagine an elastic band that wasn't flexible. No use to anyone, least of all the British people. And the British people do not like inflexible elastic bands. We demand maximum flexibility from our elastic bands, and we will continue to do so.

And we must all be flexible. Hospitals cannot stand still. Doctors cannot stand still. Patients cannot stand still. John Prescott cannot stand still. They all fidget like mad. You put one down somewhere, and the next day it's gone.

But I promise you this. From next April, there will be up to ten specially funded health action zones around the country. Their remit is threefold: to zone action health; to health-zone all action; and, perhaps most importantly, to zone all health-action.

And I pledge you this. After a year, it is our intention that a fully resourced review body will find that there is no further need for those ten specially funded health action zones. It will be a time for hard choices. Hard, compassionate choices. Tough, caring choices. And in one fell swoop, in a year's time this country will be free of those ten specially funded health action zones. Free from the chains of the health action zones. The British have never been keen on specially funded health action zones. They are not in our nature. So, a year from April, it's goodbye to specially funded health action zones. And that is my solemn pledge.

Look, our new Britain will have the same values as ever. It should be a soft, compassionate society, but it is compassion with a hard edge. I am often asked, 'How do you like your edges? Hard-boiled or soft?' And I say I like my hard edges soft. And my soft edges hard. And for this we need soldiers.

We cannot say we want a strong and secure society when we ignore its very foundation: family life. This is not about preaching to individuals about their private lives. Far from it. Their private lives are their own affair. People are free to do whatever they like. And so they should be. But we must see that they stop it, and stop it this minute.

Look, attitudes have changed. The world has changed. I am a modern man leading a modern country. I like modern songs. The Rolling Stones are a particular favourite. All Britons admire their beat and their sheer enthusiasm. But if you're going to play them so loud, would you kindly shut that door? I can't hear myself think. And let me tell you this: I won't ask you again.

A rise in teenage pregnancies; more crime; more poverty; more truancy; more neglect of educational opportunities; more unhappiness. We've achieved it before, and there's no reason why we can't achieve it again.

Again, my vision for Britain is clear. It is to make this country pivotal. In future, when the globe is spun, I want Britain to lead the way round, so that other countries are forced to follow. One thing is certain. We must not be left behind. If Europe, Asia, America are spinning, then we must spin faster, or they will overtake us.

I have a vision of Europe. My vision for Europe is clear. I want a people's Europe. And not only a people's Europe but a Europe full of people. People who share our vision. A people's vision of a people's Europe. A soft Europe, with hard edges.

Look, I know there will be a hard choice to come over a single currency. That is not something we will shirk. Our policy remains unchanged: we have already made the hardest choice. And that hard choice was not to make a hard choice until the moment for it has been and gone.

And let me say this. This and let me say. Me say and let this. I issue a challenge to each and every one of you. Unite behind our mission to modernise the country. Wherever you go in this great nation, seek to look modern, to speak modern, to be modern. Away with those old shoes. Away with those brown slacks with the underheel hoops. Away with those old long-players by The Seekers. We want a Britain of New Shoes. New Slacks. New Seekers.

On 1 May 1997, it wasn't just the Tories who were defeated. Fear itself was defeated. But I warn you this. Keep supporting us, keep voting for us – or fear will be back, worse than ever, with all sorts of horrors and unimaginable nastinesses not far behind.

Britain – Britain, heads, bodies and tails – can be unbeatable. Make the good that is in the heart of each of us serve the good of all. May your days be merry and bright. And may all your Christmases be white. Have I told you lately that I love you? Let the sunshine in, the sun shine in. How do you do what you do to me? If I only knew! If I knew what you're doing to me, I'd do it to you. Knock three times on the ceiling if you want me. Twice on the pipe if the answer is no.

Finally, I say this to you all. Look, I make no apology. We have explored every avenue. We have published details. The world has changed. Our vision is clear. The opportunity is before us. Nothing less. There is still a long way to go. But we shall seize it.

And that is an achievement to be proud of.

Appendix 3

From *Creative Britain* by Chris Smith (Faber, 1998), co-written with special creative adviser Bel Littlejohn

Put your ear to the ground. Take a good listen. Yes – Britain is positively buzzing with a hotbed of exciting benchmarks woven into the cutting edge of the common thread of the very fabric of our society and generating lively debate.

Our film industry, for instance, is positively humming. *The Full Monty* exceeded all expectations at home and abroad. And both at home and abroad *The Full Monty* exceeded all expectations. Meanwhile all expectations, both at home and abroad, were amply exceeded by *The Full Monty*.

And our exciting young modern young exciting young and exciting young modern British artists are challenging some of our most basic assumptions in a way that is young, modern and exciting. They do not shy from asking the big questions. Questions like 'What is Art?' 'Who is Art?' 'Where is Art?' and 'Will Art meet me for a drink at the Groucho tonight?'

And let's not get bogged down in arguments about whether it is 'high culture' or 'low culture' that is important here. These are misleading distinctions. Keats may not have been quite as good as Bob Dylan on the mouth-organ, but he probably had a better singing voice. Both Rostropovich and Liam Gallagher are musicians of the first rank, though at the time of writing only one of them is going out with Patsy Kensit.

The Prime Minister did indeed invite Oasis to Number 10, but a few days later he was at the Cottesloe Theatre being deeply moved by *King Lear*. And as he himself said in a highly successful photo-call with King Lear afterwards, 'I am absolutely delighted to have had this opportunity to meet and get to know King Lear and his lovely family. As you know, I have long been a great admirer of the King, and in particular the way he has come through one helluva lot of hardships on the domestic front to become a great ambassador for this country. He's a true professional.' Might I also mention in this context that *The Full Monty* is a great British success story, exceeding all expectations both at home and abroad.

E.M. Forster once said, 'Only Connect'. And it's hard not to agree with him. This is advice that continues to echo down the decades, to be repeated in speeches and books by distinguished men of affairs who simply haven't got the time on their hands to remember anything else Forster or anyone else ever said. So let's reflect today on those two little words. 'Only' – that's four letters – and 'Connect' – that's seven. Eleven letters in all. And what happens if we as a society choose to ignore Forster's advice? That's right. The missed train is missed. The plumbing proves faulty. The electric light fails to come on. And such is the power of Forster's phrase that – like *The Full Monty* – it has exceeded all expectations in the American market. One state has even considered employing it as a slogan in its marketing brochures. Only Connecticut.

And so to the Millennium. What is it about this thing called the Millennium? Why is it so important? In answer to that, I would say that on the deepest level, it is a moment in time that gives us the chance to ask some tremendously challenging questions. How did we get here? What are we doing here? Wouldn't we rather be somewhere else? Or would it be too damp? Where are we going now that we've been where we set out to go before we arrived at the place where we were when we started to wonder what we'd be doing once we had moved over there?

The Millennium Dome Experience will offer an extra-ordinary showcase for the future of a truly modern Britain. There will be moving staircases – fully automated with the very latest in modern gadgetry and able to take you both up and down – of a type only ever seen before in leading department stores and major international airports. There will be exciting light displays on a par with the very best concerts by top groups Oasis and Massive Attack. And there will be cutting-edge ice-creams and futuristic toys without cutting edges available in the foyer. We are also hoping to hire a screen and show the top British movie *The Full Monty* – a film whose well-deserved success has, inci-dentally, radically exceeded all expectations.

A word or too, also, about the National Lottery. The Lottery has proved to be something from which millions of people derive genuine fun. What could be more fun than spending a pound or two on a lottery ticket and waiting in expectation and trepidation for the rest of the week for the news to come through that you are now a multi-millionaire and then tuning in on Saturday night to watch those seven little balls rolling into place and discovering that – hey presto! – not a single one matches the numbers on your card and instead of being a multi-millionaire you are now worse off than you were before! It's a game that continues to give a lot of pleasure to countless millions, and countless millions to the board of Camelot.

This Government has harnessed and will continue to harness the extraordinarily diverse and exciting young modern young exciting energy that is evident not only in films such as *The Full Monty* but also in many other areas of the arts and entertainment – in that great British success *The Full Monty*, for instance. The Tower of London, Hadrian's Wall, Waterloo Bridge, The Forth Bridge – these are all exciting new monuments to this Government's unwavering

239

commitment to the arts. And it's an open secret that Liam Gallagher, Damien Hirst, Sir Elton John and the cast of *The Full Monty* have all driven over Waterloo Bridge during the course of the past eighteen months.

In planting Stonehenge earlier this year, we have set out to make a new, exciting and modern arena – both challenging and stimulating – accessible on an unprecedented scale to the great diversity of ordinary British people. No doubt the cynics would say that it is no more than a collection of old stones. But to them I say this. The Prime Minister has already visited Stonehenge, and has been photographed mixing on a one-to-one basis with some of the senior stones. By the end of this century, we aim to have made Stonehenge wholly interactive, with moving staircases and cutting-edge laser shows, and to be marketing it with its own distinctive logo.

Already, we have seen a creative explosion in this country, celebrating our past as well as our future. From Damien Hirst's 'What's the hell's the point of carrying on breathing?' to 'You Want Your Head Kicked In?' by The Prodigy, all the way through to that highly successful upbeat British film about unemployed steelworkers who spend a night stripping before going back on the dole, British artists are setting new standards of enthusiasm in communicating their sheer, unbounded joy in being alive in Britain today. Hear that buzz! Let's boogie!

Index

242

243

245